Free
to be a
Princess

Self-Esteem Bible Study for Women

Lesia Glick

Unless other wise noted all scripture quotations are taken from the New International Version of the Bible.

Scripture quotation is taken from The Comparative Study Bible
©1984 by The Zondervan Corporation

The New International Version
©1973, 1978, 1984 by International Bible Society

The Amplified Bible
©1965

ISBN: [09771931-0-1]

Printed in the United States of America

Dedication

*I dedicate this study in all that it is and all
that it is to become to my Lord and Savior, Jesus Christ.*

*I also dedicate this study to my wonderful husband Gail,
whom I adore and my three children Justin, Rebekah, and Kevin.*

*And to Pastors Eric and Gena Boggs who have poured so
much into my life and instilled vision in me that I never dreamed of.*

Table of Contents

Forward

What a beautiful revelation of God's love, purpose, and plan for all of His lovely creation – "Free to Be a Princess Self-Esteem Bible Study for Women". This is more than another study. This is a life-changing, life-enhancing, revelation of the truth in God's Word! In this study, the schemes of the enemy that have been set up against self-esteem and self-worth are revealed.

We remember the first time Lesia shared with us the first steps of the knowledge and revelation she received from God's Word concerning self-esteem. As we journeyed through the pages of her script, the presence and anointing of God was so real that we wept as we read. There was never any doubt that what Lesia had written was divinely inspired by God the Father, the Creator and Lover of our souls. We have seen the reality of the word that God has revealed in this study lived out in Lesia's life.

Lesia has been obedient to God and has had a listening ear to His voice as she penned the words of this study. She has explored God's written Word and listened to His Word in her heart. In fact God is using Lesia, not only through this study she has written, but also in our local church. This is evidence of her daily pursuit of God. She has walked the "recovery to self-esteem" road herself. She has overcome trials and walked through the enemy's schemes that were intended to destroy her life and her family. She has walked through the many processes that have led to growth and maturity in the Lord and now God is using her to touch the lives of women everywhere. Her heart for God is shown in her love for His people and in her concern for their growth and realization of God's destiny for their lives.

God has used Lesia in a mighty way through this study. We personally know scores of women whose lives have been changed forever after going through the "Free to Be a Princess" study. However, as we examine God's word and this study, we understand that what God has done for Lesia and for many others, He desires to do for all men, women, boys, and girls everywhere. It is God's will that each us realize our place in Christ, realize the fact that we are "fearfully and wonderfully made" and realize that we can be free to pursue God and His plan for our lives without reservation! Each of us can be "Free to Be a Princess" and free to be everything God has called us to be!

In Christ,

Pastors Eric and Gena Boggs
Beech Springs Tabernacle, Senior Pastors

My Prayer for You

How to use this study.

This book is designed to be a workbook and journal within a Bible study. In this study, you'll step into His word as you embark on a journey of discovering who you are and your true- esteem in Christ. As you go through this book you will find yourself growing as an individual and growing closer to God with each step you take. I encourage you to take your time with each step and be honest; things may get messy, but the end result will be worth it. Before you start take a moment to flip through the book to familiarize yourself with the steps. Be sure to take advantage of the journaling, reflections and prayer times as they will help you walk through the steps of self-esteem healing and freedom. Each step leads you to the true freedom that awaits you as a Princess of God.

I pray that as you step into your Free to Be a Princess journey that it will bring defining moments in your life that will forever change you. I pray that as you hold this book in your hand you surrender to the work of the Holy Spirit. I pray that your heart and mind be an open vessel for the Holy Spirit to mold into a free Princess of God. I believe that this is a divine appointment in your life.

Father God, I pray that you would guide my sister, lift her head, and show her truth in your word about who she is. I pray that in her brokenness she will be liberated to rise up and overcome. I believe in your work and asked it to be sealed with each step she takes closer to you. Lead her to the freedom you died to give her, so that she may be the free Princess you have purposed her to be. In Jesus name Amen.

Preface

God has walked me through so much in my life, never leaving me nor forsaking me. Because of Him and His faithfulness, I have freedom in Him today! I haven't always known or felt secure about God's love, faithfulness, and grace, until God walked with me through self-esteem recovery.

As the author of this book, God has called me to share some of my life so that it will help you and bring glory to Him. Many things I share in this testimony are not easy to write, but the truth is I'm a real person who had real issues to work through. Because of the grace of God, I've recovered from low self-esteem. If sharing my life will help one of you recover, then it has all been worth it! It is my desire to bring glory to my Heavenly Father through my testimony and share His restoration, healing, and love that was given to me.

> *I praise God because I am fearfully and wonderfully made; your works are wonderful, I know that full well!*
>
> *– Psalms 139:14*

Childhood Issues

I could share so much, but I'll hit the highlights to give you glimpse into my past of self-esteem struggles and pains. Many times it's the people you love that cause great wounds in your self-esteem. I don't play the blame game, but I do know the enemy can use people to hurt and bring pain to others.

My self-esteem struggles started when I was young. I didn't understand everything about self-esteem; I just knew that I didn't think I had much worth. Many times during my childhood, people would say things to me that would crush my spirit. I felt like a failure many times.

Because of the insecurities I developed as a young girl, I created the need to be validated and affirmed by someone else. I never felt good enough. I was never encouraged in school, didn't make good grades, and didn't feel smart. I always compared myself to my younger brother. He seemed to always be the one who was everyone's favorite. Even during my college years, I was still seeking someone to accept and approve of me. It was a struggle to know who Lesia was.

I had been saved as a child, but I didn't have a real relationship with Jesus. I knew that there was something missing. As I got older, I sought more for validation and self-worth in all of the wrong places. I looked for acceptance from my high school boyfriend. I found out how quickly you can stray away from the things that you know are right.

Who Would Have Thought

I went to college to prove that I could do it, and I could be somebody. I never took the time to ask God what He wanted to do with my life. I left college my junior year to marry my high school boyfriend. I didn't know if this was the person I was supposed to marry or not. I now realized that I married who was supposed to be my best friend, not my husband.

The first year of our marriage was good, but things changed. I was still searching for self-worth and validation that I so much needed. During the second year of our marriage, the bomb was dropped.

There were secret issues that I discovered about him that started a downward spiral to destruction. These issues affected his job, so he had no choice but to tell me. I felt like there was a whole other secret lifestyle going on, and I didn't have a clue!

He lost his job, was publicly humiliated, and had to admit to me things that no man would want to have to admit to his wife. Things were broadcasted on the television and in the paper that brought shame and embarrassment to both of us. The embarrassment was overwhelming!

Searching for Answers

Although this was very hard to take, I accepted it and attempted to get some restoration for the marriage. To no avail, things kept getting worse, and issues kept rising. There was one lie after another, and suddenly I realized I had absolutely no idea what the truth was about our marriage. My trust for him was gone. I realized my husband (at the time) had serious issues that I had adopted as my own, but I needed to realize that I didn't commit the actions that He did. It was time for me to move forward to straighten myself out. It was not my fault that he secretly sought others outside of marriage.

My self-esteem was shattered. I felt no self-worth and no love. Here I was with a failed marriage, college dropout, and clueless of who I was. I felt like a total failure.

I had a precious little boy who came at what seemed to be such an odd time, but it was a perfect time. He brought much love, peace, and joy into my life when I was going through some of my toughest times. If it were not for that little boy, there would have many times I would have just quit altogether on everything. God's timing is so good even when we don't understand it. I weep as I write this and think about what hurt and pain I used to have, but yet I have made it through.

Divorce is a tragedy and very damaging to all who go through it. God hates divorce not the divorcee (That should free a lot of you that have been through one). I know what it's like to face divorce and live alone as a single Mom. The struggle was hard, and I found myself at another place where I was searching for answers.

Who Am I

I had no idea who I was or what I was supposed to be. I went through depression, loneliness, anger, bitterness, and financial struggles. I found myself very angry with a hateful attitude. I got to the point that I didn't like myself; I was being led by circumstance and not truth. I had declared that I hated men, but I found myself seeking out validation and someone to make my self-esteem feel better. I got involved in a very unhealthy relationship that was not even like me. I was trying to fill the emptiness inside.

I struggled with my identity. After all I had been through, I really felt like a nobody. It was my lowest point of self-worth and value with no sure identity. Shame and guilt came because I did things that I knew that I didn't need to do. This added to the self-esteem issues that I already had.

Redemption

It wasn't until I traveled through all of these really hard times that I turned my life around and went back to the one thing I needed most – Jesus! I rededicated my life to Him and from that moment on things begin to change in my life. I made many mistakes, but in His grace and mercy He continued to love and pursue me. I never once had to prove myself to Him. He loved me unconditionally.

All my life, I looked for others to validate me. I was always searching for acceptance, yet feeling condemned like a failure. When I sold my life out to Jesus Christ, He started the healing process in me. I had to make a decision. I gave God all of my mess, hurts, shame, guilt and condemnation. When I surrendered all to him, I began to change.

He touched me in a special way by filling me with JOY! By the infilling of the Holy Spirit, I had a laugh and a joy that I had never known before. I remember for a long time I would just laugh in the Spirit. I know that God gave me joy and restored my smile!

All of this change in my life did not happen over night. It took years for His work to bring victory in my life. Many times we want God to heal us quickly, but to experience God's healing is to grow closer to Jesus with every step. I found out that I was beautiful, and He had beautiful things in store for me. He revealed my gifts, talents, and purpose. He taught me how to follow Him. I began to desire freedom. I was no longer looking for someone to make me feel special.

When You Are Not Looking

God placed a wonderful Christian man right in front of me, when I wasn't looking. As we dated, I found that I was truly scared of a relationship. This man was great for me, and God had sent him my way. I tried to run away, but he kept pursuing! Because of my fears and anxiety of past hurts from men, I nearly missed what God was trying to do. I received counseling from my Pastor. I thought it was too good to be true! I am now married to that wonderful man, Gail, and I praise God for Him (We have been married seven years)!

When Will It End

I found myself dealing with issues again. Here I was with a new love seeking validation from him and still never realizing the degree of my low self-esteem and self-worth. Gail and I both had been through divorces and difficult times afterwards.

We worked through our issues together to remove them from our marriage. When you have been married before it is imperative to be open and honest and recover from the previous divorce. Nothing of the old marriage can be brought into the new one and that includes old baggage and misconceptions about marriage. It's important not to compare or analyze. Release the old, start fresh.

Though we were open and honest with each other, the enemy used emotions, past hurts, and recorded messages to rise up at the worst times. He can replay things in your mind, and before you realize it, you are taking it out on your new love!

Determined to be Healed

We were determined to have a marriage that God would be the third chord. We met at church and were sold out to God, but there was more for us in marriage than what we were experiencing. We knew that in our marriage we had to go after God with

> *A chord of three strands is not quickly torn apart.*
>
> – Ecclesiastes 4:12

all that we had. We realized that we did not know how to have a marriage with God as the center. We had been through such tough times; we didn't know how to communicate or respect the others feelings. I had a hard time! Even though I had begun the healing process of my self-esteem, I didn't realize I had a self esteem problem until God revealed it to me. I just thought I was supposed to feel the way I did and deal with it. I was looking for Gail to build me up and make me feel valuable. I wanted him to esteem me! Here I was again in the struggle trying to fill a need the wrong way.

In God's sweet love, He began to take me to His word. He would take me to scriptures that would validate who I was in Him. God told me specifically to stop looking to Gail to make my self-esteem what it is supposed to be. He said Lesia, "I will make your self-esteem what it should be. I am the One you need to seek for love and validation. Stop looking to other people when what you need is in Me. Do not look to your husband for your self-esteem; you'll never get it." I realized that I was putting undo pressure on Gail because of my low self-esteem. So, ladies, stop looking to your husband to fill every need. Most of my self-esteem issues had nothing to do with my husband. I had deep self-esteem issues from my previous marriage, and yet I expected Gail to fix me. He was not God of my life, and He couldn't fix me!!

I wanted a compliment or to be affirmed from my husband, so badly, but he wouldn't do it. That is just not in his make-up. Later, I realized that God knew what I needed in a mate. He knew that I didn't need somebody to constantly affirm me because He wanted me to allow Him to encourage and affirm me. God wanted first place, so I would look to Him first. Don't get me wrong, compliments and encouragements are good, but you don't have to have them for every little thing! He gave me so much in my husband. God gave me a very faithful, hard-working man that has a heart for Him. Gail is the leader of our marriage, and the load lifted off my shoulders. We see now how we compliment one another. What he is lacking I have and vice versa!

Whole In Christ

Now I know that God affirms me, and Gail chooses to compliment me more often. I know who I am in Christ! God affirms me daily in my quiet time with His word and by the Holy Spirit. Jesus will meet your every need and heal all the brokenness that you have ever felt! Jesus will fill all of the empty places in your life and fill you with a joy that you don't understand! That is how good He is. He did that for me, and He will do that for you!

God spoke to me through every study, book, or service I was involved in, and

His word became real in my life. He even sent people to encourage and share the word with me. My pastors have always encouraged people to be who they are in Him. They let our church body know that we are valuable and have purpose. That truth took deep roots in my spirit, and with the help of the Holy Spirit, I knew that I was valuable with purpose.

My past didn't matter to God; He still had a plan for my life from the very beginning. He showed me truth in His Word. I know who I am in Jesus Christ! He showed me that I am His princess, and that I am special to Him. He loves me unconditionally. He showed me that when Jesus sacrificed His life on the cross He thought of me. He thought of my self-esteem, and He did not die on the cross for me to live defeated and discouraged with a low self-esteem. He gave his all, so I could live free and in victory.

New Season

I was able to quit my full time job and go back to college. I earned my Bachelor of Science degree. I wanted to teach full-time; however, the Lord had different plans for me. With the birth of my daughter, came the call to be a stay-at-home Mom. I always worked and had something to do. I had to adjust to being a stay-at-home mom with no one around. Again, I felt so insignificant until the Lord revealed His purpose for me. First and foremost

I am His child, then a wife, and then a mother. Everything else falls in place after that. I went through the battle of being just a Mom or just a housewife. No one is "just" anything. God has a specific call and plan for all of us. I know that God brings different seasons into our lives to fulfill the plan, but yet I felt so alienated from people that I struggled with my self-esteem. People and family made comments like, "I can not believe you went to college, and now you are not teaching! You are just wasting your degree. I can not believe that you are sitting at home!" Well, God had to give me great revelation to overcome these attacks. Once again He took me to His word to show me how valuable I am as a mother. I am called to be a wife and mother. Motherhood is my career. I know that I am doing what God wants me to despite what others say. I love always being there for my husband and children. It is so rewarding, even though it didn't feel that way at first.

In the time that I have been a stay-at-home Mom, I have had the opportunity to watch my children accomplish their milestones that I would have missed. Being a mom and wife is valuable. Do not lessen your worth because you don't work or make an income. This time at home has not only blessed my family, but I've grown spiritually. I am more involved with my church and can minister to others more frequently. This may not have been possible had I worked. Now in my life, I can experience the true peace of God because I'm doing what He has called me to do.

My freedom has been a 10 year process that begun when I rededicated my life to Jesus. I know now that God loves me and has a purpose for me. There is no greater freedom than the healing and peace that comes from a healthy self-esteem that has been touched by Jesus. He showed me how to walk in love, forgiveness, and trust in Him to lead the way. As I freely received His forgiveness, I was able to forgive myself and those who hurt me.

It's Your Turn

Will it be easy? No. A lot of hurt is deep rooted and may be very painful to face. No matter how painful it is, Jesus will carry you through. There is freedom in Him.

You can live free today because of the love of Jesus Christ. He has redeemed and restored you. There may be struggles, but you will know who you are in Jesus Christ. You can be free to be yourself. You are a beautiful princess of God who is fearfully and wonderfully made. Like me, you are a masterpiece! Like the Psalmist said, *I know that full well!*

Where Am I Now

I now have three children, two boys and a girl. I am blessed! I live as a happy woman and in peace. I serve as the Women's Ministries Director of my church where I encourage and teach women to be all they are called to be. My heart's passion is for women to know their value and identity in Christ. If someone would have told me 10 years ago I would be doing this, I would have told them they were nuts! If I knew I would be writing a Bible study and sharing my testimony, I would have probably laughed.

I believe that this is all part of His great plan for me. God can always take what the enemy means for harm and turn it into something beautiful that will bring glory to His name. Look what the Lord has done in me!

Step One
Your Father, Your Creator

As this journey of self-esteem freedom and healing begins, the first step is to meet your Heavenly Father. You are going to discover who your Creator is. You say "What does this have to do with my self-esteem?" Everything! You need to know who He is in His mighty power and glory. You must realize and understand that He created you with a plan, and He needs total control of your life. When you can see who He is and that He spoke you into being "for such a time as this", then you can begin to move into receiving your healing from the Father.

You must first know who your Father is in order to know who you are. This is the first step in the journey of your self-esteem healing. You are to come to *the Father* to get to know Him more intimately. In 1 Peter 5:7, His word says, *To cast all your anxiety on Him because he cares for you.* He is waiting for you to bring everything to him, and He will take care of it all, even your self-esteem.

The time has come for you to see who you really are. It is the time to seek His face and meet your Creator to discover your purpose and receive all that is yours. Now is the time to begin to reach deep within you and allow the "princess" in you to come forth. You can learn to talk with your Abba Father (Daddy) about some of the struggles, hurts, and defeat that keep you from feeling like and being the princess of God you are called to be! No longer are you to walk in defeat or fear with low self-esteem. You are God's princess, and He wants to heal and help you to realize who you really are in Him.

> *For you did not receive a spirit that makes you slave again to fear, But you received the spirit of sonship. And by him we cry "Abba Father". The Spirit himself testifies with our spirit that we are God's children. Now if we are children, Then we are heirs - heirs of God And co-heirs with Christ.*
>
> – Romans 8:15-17

Day 1

Abba Father–
"Daddy"

All throughout the life of people, God is often seen as a father figure. He is compared to what is seen in our earthly father of which may or may not be a good example. As you began this journey of self-esteem healing, I want you to lay aside all your views about a father. You are going to see your heavenly Father for who He is. It is a time that every woman comes to know her Abba, Father, her Daddy, who created her (Abba is the Aramaic word for "Daddy").

Your Father in heaven is calling you to get to know Him in a more intimate way. His arms are opened wide inviting you to come and rest in His presence. He wants to hold you close and walk you through the healing of your self-esteem. He wants you to rise up and be a new woman today! No matter what walk of life you come from, God is your Father, and He cares for you. He is waiting to pour out His compassion on you simply because you are His daughter.

Read and write Psalms 103:13-14 (I like writing the verses because it makes you focus and read it carefully. It allows more time to get in your spirit. I encourage you to write the verses as we go. It will greatly benefit you.).

Read and write Psalms 68:5-6.

Where do you fit in with God?

Are you without a father?

Are you lonely?

Are you surrounded by people, but yet live a lonely life?

Are you carrying around weights of the past that hold you back from living free?

Do you live under condemnation of mistakes and sins you have committed?

Have you alienated yourself because of your past sins?

Do you ever feel like no one loves or cares about you?

Do you really know who you are and your purpose?

Do you feel special?

No matter what your answers may be to any of the previous questions, God cares for you. You no longer have to live with the chains of a prisoner due to low or poor self-esteem. Your Daddy in heaven desires to show you compassion like you have never known before. He will lead you to freedom from a low self-esteem.

Throughout this step I want you to get to know your Creator. I hope that you will see how much He loves and cares for you. He created you, and you are His daughter, His princess!

Prayer Time

Dear Heavenly Father,

Thank you that you are my Daddy in heaven. Please help me to see you and come to know you like never before. Please help me to see myself as your daughter. Please help me to understand how important I am to you. O Lord, I surrender myself self-esteem to you as I begin this study. Reveal to me your healing touch and your glory. Help me, Lord, to know that I am special to you and that I am your princess, in Jesus name. – Amen

Use the space provided throughout the book to write your own prayers.

Time to Journal

I want you to take time right now to stop and recognize your heavenly Father, your Abba Father - Daddy. Think about His place in your life and what He means to you. Write your responses below.

■■ Explain how you have always viewed God.

_____

_____

_____

_____

■■ Where does God fit into your life today?

_____

_____

_____

_____

■■ At this point in your life, who or what do you need God to be or do for you?

_____

_____

_____

_____

_____

_____

Day 2

Meet Your Creator

In the beginning God created the heavens and the earth.

– Genesis 1:1

*Now the earth **was formless and empty, and darkness** was over the surface of the deep, and the Spirit of God was hovering over the waters.*

– Genesis 1:2

God is your Creator. He is the only Creator. You have probably heard the creation story many, many times. Have you ever stopped to really think about it? It is often a story that is many take for granted never realizing the splendor and majestic power of God. He is the only Creator. There is nothing that can be done any greater than what God has already done and can do.

Webster's dictionary defines the word *create as "to bring into being"*. God your Creator brought everything that is "into being". How awesome is that for a Father? You have a Father who created it all. He brought everything that is into being and had a plan in mind for all He created. When the earth was without form, God decided to shape it into something beautiful.

There was nothing, and God began to speak and bring everything that is into creation. He took something that was formless and dark, and spoke His creation into being. That shows His awesome power. His power testifies to what He can do with your spirit when you allow Him to enter into the dark and empty places in your life. He will fill it with something beautiful!

▪▪ **Special reading:** Take the time to read on your own Genesis 1. Meditate on how He created and what He created right from the beginning. Look at His power and His creative thoughts that are so above ours. The Bible says in Isaiah 55:8, *For my thoughts are not your thoughts, neither are your ways my ways.* His creative plan is so above anything that we can only begin to imagine.

▪▪ Read and write Genesis 1:26-27. (Go ahead and read it aloud a few times.)

_____

_____

_____

_____

_____

Did you hear what you just read? Imagine God in His splendor stopping for a moment, after He looks at His beautiful creation, and saying those verses. You are made in the image of God and "image" includes His characteristics. His image includes characteristics of His righteousness, holiness, knowledge, and every spiritual blessing He has for us. God even goes on to say that you will rule over all the earth.

⠿ Read and write Psalms 8:5-6.

_____

_____

_____

_____

You were made the ruler over all else, and you are important. At times one only thinks of His creation when standing on a mountain top gazing into the horizon as far as the eye can see. Or, standing on the beach while watching the sunrise over the ocean and experiencing the newness of the day. What you can fail to realize is how much more he created when He created you. His greatest creation is not the earth and its beauty, but His greatest creation came when He created man in "His" image and nothing else compares. In Genesis 1:27, it says that *So God created man in His own image,* and by doing so, you must realize the stamp of God on your life. Therefore, as a woman you must realize that when God created woman, you were created in His image. The verse reads *man was created in His Image,* but that includes male and female. You have that same stamp of God Himself!

Read this verse again, and let it soak into your heart.

· **Genesis 1:27:** *So God created man in His own image, the image of God He created him; male and female He created them.*

· **Genesis 1:31:** *God saw all that He made and it was very good.*
  *Read this aloud a few times.

God, your Creator, saw what He had completed, and He liked it! There is more to this; read on. Remember you are on a journey to a destination.

Read and write Genesis 2:18.

_____

_____

_____

_____

God says it is not good for man to be alone. He created a suitable helper for him. He says "I will make", in other words, God says, I will create, bring into being, a suitable helper. He created woman! He brought her forth in all her glory. He knew what she would be before He created her. He designed her! He fashioned her to be what He desired in His image. God, your heavenly Father, thought about you! He created you just as He wanted you for such a time as this. If He wanted you to be something different, He would have made you what He wanted. You could have been a beautiful rose in a garden, a bird or even a fish, but "no". He created you a woman! When God created woman, it was the completion of all of His creation.

We must also realize that we were created to be a suitable helper, and we must realize the importance and value in that title of "helper". The realization of this will greatly boost your self-esteem when you realize exactly who God intended for you to be. A woman is so important to man that God created her to be His "helper". Since God thought to create her for this position and called her "helper", she has an important call on her life, and she must fulfill her purpose. The title of helper is often misunderstood as being second-rate or an aid or assistant, but that is just not so. We must come to accept who God called us to be and move forward. We need to strive to be just what He says. Accept your place and allow the Holy Spirit to grow you into being a "suitable helper". We also need to see that Jesus was labeled a "helper" (Hebrews 13:6). We are called to be imitators of God (Ephesians 5:1), and that is what we should strive for. We, as women, help complete the incomplete in man (just as man completes woman). God has us positioned for purpose in His kingdom. God created us with a plan and a purpose. Accept and enjoy who and where you are. _Be_ the best helper ever!

The first woman created was Eve. You, as a woman, are no less special than Eve. You are His creation just the same as Eve. He created you, and you are good! He created a masterpiece when He created you. You may not see yourself as a beautiful masterpiece. Well, it is time for a new way of thinking! Isaiah 43:19 says, *See, I am doing a new thing!* God created you to be a beautiful masterpiece, and it is time for you to rise up and be just that. You can only do that through Him, and allowing the Holy Spirit to be *our* "helper", and follow His guidance.

Prayer Time

Dear Heavenly Father,

Thank you, Lord, for creating man and woman. Thank you, Lord that you created us in your image. Please help me change the way I see myself from this point on because I am made in your image. Thank you, Lord that I have your stamp on my life. I am unique. There is none other like me, and I thank you that you have a purpose for me as a woman. Thank you, Lord that you created me as a helper and gave me a special call, in Jesus name. – Amen

Time to Journal

▪▪ As a woman in the world today, how does it make you feel to be called a "helper"?

_____

_____

_____

_____

▪▪ What mindsets about being a helper has the world created for you about being a woman and being a "helper"?

_____

_____

_____

_____

▪▪ What steps can you take today to begin to be a better "helper" and answer the call that God has called you to?

_____

_____

_____

_____

Time to Journal

:: How does the fact that Jesus is called a "helper" make you feel about being a woman that was created to be a "helper"? Explain your feelings.

In God's eyes, He created woman to be a "helper" to man and to all. Begin to reflect on the words below that are attributes of a woman, a "helper".

Apply these words to your self-esteem.

Purposeful	Stamped with the fingerprint of God	Caregiver
Compassionate	Supporter	Emotional Communicator
Made in His Image	Love	Friend of God
Encourager	Princess	Gifted

We must remember that although God created woman to be a "helper" to man, God placed man to also be a "helper" to woman. One does not function independently without the other. Man and woman each have different God-given roles that must be fulfilled.

Day 3

Who Can I
Create?

I hope that you are now beginning to catch a glimpse of your uniqueness and preciousness to God. Today this step will take you to one of my most favorite scriptures passages in the Bible. These passages of scripture that you will read today will be one that reveals new insight as to who you are. It opened the door for freedom in my own life, and I believe it will do the same for you.

Let's go back to the word again to see what He says about you. God created every being, and He knew them and that includes you. God is the Creator of all, and He created you with so much care and decision. It is like He stopped to think, "Who can I create, and what do I want her to be?"

∷ Read and write Psalms 139:13.

_____

_____

_____

_____

It says God created you in your mother's womb. You are His creation, and He chose to give you to your mother and father as a gift. He knew you long before you were ever thought of by your earthly parents. Isn't that amazing! He goes on to say that He knitted you together in your mother's womb. That verse tells you that He knew what He was doing. God knew right from the start, the color of your hair, eyes, and skin. He shaped your face and your body to His plan. He knew what He was depositing in you, and He knew the plan He had for you at that very moment. Everything you will ever need God placed it within you when He created you. Jeremiah 29:11 tells us that _He has a plan for our lives._ God just didn't create women to go through life without a plan or a purpose. He had a plan for you the very moment He created you.

∷ Read and write Psalms 139:14.

_____

_____

Imagine God in His splendor sitting on His throne thinking of who He could create next. Then God thinks of you, and the plan He has for you. There you are, created by the Most High God. Remember, everything that He creates is good! In the NIV Bible, the last part of that verse says *I know that full well.* Ask yourself. "Do I really believe and know Psalms 139:14 to be true in me?"

Read and write Psalms 139:15-16.

Read the passage Psalm 139:13-16 again, and write what each verse says you.

Verse 13

Verse 14

Verse 15

Verse 16

No matter how or where you were made, God has a masterpiece plan for you. He knew you first, and He gave you as a gift to your mother and father. Now you may say that your parents didn't treat you as special as you are, and you may have a lot of hurt or damaged emotions by your earthly parents; however, the Holy Spirit will help you to deal with that in time. Take a step of faith and trust God by allowing God to give you a new perspective on life and how you see yourself. Right now, I want you to see your Creator. See God for His wonderful works in creating *you!* You are special, if for right now you can not find any other reason than because God created *you!*

⁛ Read and write Ecclesiastes 11:5.

Step One
Your Father, Your Creator

In the human mind, God's creation is hard to comprehend. No one knows the path of the wind nor can one try to even fathom what God's plan is. There is so much that one can not understand about life. Even within your self-esteem, you probably have often thought a lot about the "why". "Why did He create me to look the way I look?" "Why am I this way or that?" You know what I am talking about.

It is time that you change the way you think about yourself; after all, you are God's creation. Who are you to talk about what He has created? Begin to honor God with your words and thoughts about you. Begin to speak new words to yourself that will encourage you and your self-esteem. There is so much power in your words. Your mindsets can hold you back more than you know.

Later on in the study, you will deal with words and mindsets, but it is never too early to start the changing process. God created you special, and it is time for you to confess what an awesome work you are because of Him. Start right now to change your perspective. Honor your Creator and trust in Him for whom you are and praise Him because you are *fearfully and wonderfully made* by the hand of God.

Prayer Time

Dear Heavenly Father,

Thank you, Lord that I am fearfully and wonderfully made. Thank you, Lord that you knew me in my mother's womb, and you designed and knew me first and foremost. Please help me, Lord, to see myself the way you desire me too. Please help me to know who I am full well because I am created by your hand. Begin today to change my perspective about myself. Change my words and thoughts that are not pleasing to you. I realize that I am your creation in whom you are pleased, in Jesus name. – Amen

Day 4

His Princess – His Masterpiece

God, your Father, is the potter and you belong to Him, and what He created is good. You, my dear friend, are God's handiwork. There is not one woman that God, the Potter, has created that He is not pleased with His creation. You are like clay in His hands, and He molds you to be just what He purposes. He didn't stop creating good things back in the book of Genesis. He is still the Creator today. When He created you He brought forth a beautiful masterpiece, and it is good!

You must start right now by fully believing in what His word says about you. Allow the Holy Spirit to show you how special you are to God. Grab hold to the Father and realize how special you are to Him just because you are *you!* Realizing your uniqueness and preciousness to God will be the start of a healthy self-esteem. It is time that you realize the woman you are in Christ, and let the Holy Spirit heal and restore what has been lost. There is obtainable healing through Christ if you will just receive.

Read and write Isaiah 64:8.

_____

_____

_____

_____

_____

Read and write Ephesians 2:10.

_____

_____

_____

_____

_____

Once again God's word tells us that we are His workmanship, created by His hands. You were created by Him, and you are His masterpiece, His beautiful work that He made good. The Amplified Bible says, *For we are God's [own] handiwork (His workmanship) recreated in Christ Jesus...* (Ephesians 2:10). This verse could just stand alone in telling women that they were created by the hand of God to be a masterpiece. Not only were you as a woman created to be a masterpiece, but you were created to do well! It is a fact that God created you good and for you to do well; therefore, it is time to accept the fact that you are *good!*

Prayer Time

Dear Heavenly Father,

Thank you that I have been created as a beautiful masterpiece. I must confess that I have not always felt like a masterpiece or felt good about myself. I am now at a new point in my life, and I choose to think differently about myself. Please, Lord, shape me and mold me into the woman you desire me to be. Shape my self-esteem to be what you purposed it to be, in Jesus name. – Amen

Day 5
More Than A Conqueror

All throughout this step, you will go straight to God's word to look at your Creator and who He created. I believe there is no better source to enhance the work of the Holy Spirit than to read His word. I not only want you to read His word, I want you to meditate on and believe His word. The more you read, the stronger you will become. When attacks come to make you feel less than you are, you can recall what the Bible says. It is hard for things to come against you when you are standing fully on His word and you know what it says. Knowledge of God's word builds God-confidence.

There is no book or study that will help you more than God's word. I could write ten different studies, but if you never read the Bible and let His word get deep into your heart and mind, then none of them will help. God desires for you to have a healthy self-esteem. I know that because He led me to write this study for women. He has done so much for me, and He will do the same for you. Everything you will do and experience in this study God has already completed it in me. I will always be a work in progress as He works on me everyday. I will become what He wants me to be!

These verses are crucial for you. You may even want to memorize this one.

Read and write Romans 8:37-39.

_____

_____

_____

_____

You are more than a conqueror in Christ. There is nothing that shall separate you from the love of God. He knows all about your faults, weaknesses, and failures. He is aware of the guilt, shame, you carry over your past, yet, He loves you regardless. As a matter of fact, when you asked for forgiveness, He forgot all about them. It may be you that is still holding on to old stuff, and He is waiting for you to come to Him and let Him take all of your cares. With Christ, you can have a healthy self-esteem. God created you to be good and no matter what life has brought your way, you can still be the woman God intended you to be. Allow God to work through this study to fill your dark and empty places, your wounds, and your self-esteem with the beauty of Christ. My prayer, for you, is that you come to know who you are in Christ.

Prayer Time

Dear Heavenly Father,

Thank you, Lord for all that you have revealed to me. I praise you, Lord, for your wonderful work. Lord, help me begin to believe and live like a conqueror. I realize that with Jesus Christ, I am more than a conqueror. Please help me to walk and live conquering a low self-esteem, in Jesus name! – Amen

Reflection

Read through this passage and fill your name in the blanks. Then I want you to go back and read it several times aloud. Keep reading it daily as we move through this journey of the healing process.

I, _____, was created by God. He sat on His throne and thought about me. He planned everything within _____ because I am His daughter. His word says He created my innermost being. He knitted me together in my mother's womb. I praise Him because I, _____ , am fearfully and wonderfully made. I, _____ , am a masterpiece created by my heavenly Father, my Abba Father. My Daddy in heaven created me as a wonderful masterpiece and placed me as a gift to my mother and father here on earth. Although, my life may not have stayed on the correct path and I may have made some wrong choices, God still loves me. No matter what has happened in my life I, _____, am still special to God. I am a beautiful masterpiece God created, and I am full of potential to be the beautiful woman of God he intends for me to be. From this day forward I, _____, will walk in what God purposed me to be. I am a masterpiece!

:: *EXERCISE*

Go to a mirror with pen and paper in hand. As you stand in this mirror, begin to look at what you see. Notice every detail of God's handiwork and began to write it down on your paper. Start at the top of your head and work your way down. Discover your uniqueness that is only special to you. (Example: your long eyelashes, clear blue eyes, the hands, and so on.)

Reflection

Time to Journal

Write a letter to God. Start your letter as a thank you note to God for creating you. Pour your heart out to God about how you truly see yourself. Be honest with yourself and with God. This is part of your healing and restoration process. God already knows, but it brings forth freedom when you begin to admit how you feel and surrender it to Him.

Dear God,

_____

_____

_____

_____

_____

_____

_____

_____

_____

_____

_____

_____

_____

_____

_____

_____

_____

Love,
Your Princess _____

Step Two
Salvation – Your Gift!

God is an awesome God! He is the creator of all things and the Creator of good things. As you studied in the previous step, you know you are God's workmanship; *you* are His Masterpiece! God knew exactly what He was doing with His creation, and He was not without a plan. *God knows the plan He has for your life* (Jeremiah 29:11), and He also knows that in your life, *you would face troubles, trials, and temptation* (John 16:33). He knows that the enemy, *Satan, is roaming around like a roaring lion to destroy us* (1 Peter 5:8). He knows the enemy is trying to scheme up a plan to destroy you, but God has a bigger plan. His plan provides a way of escape from what Satan wants to be. *God created His Son, Jesus Christ, to be an atoning sacrifice for all to be saved from destruction* (1 John 2:2). He knew that all of us would need a Savior, and He created a perfect man to come to earth and walk among men. *He experienced life as you and I live, and He sinned not* (Hebrews 4:15). It is awesome to think that the same God that created me also created Jesus, our Savior. God had a plan in mind when Jesus was just a babe born in a manger. John 3:16 tells us that *God gave his only Son so that no one would perish,* and that includes you and me. He created His son Jesus and sent Him to the cross just so you and I could be free.

My dear friend, it is God's will for you to come to know Jesus Christ as your Lord and Savior. Salvation is part of God's ultimate plan for your life. My question to you today is, "Where do you stand in your relationship with Christ?" Do you know Him as your Savior? Do you personally know Jesus or just know about Him?

I want you to take this time right now and think about your relationship with Him. Do you have a personal relationship with Him? God desires that you know Him. He wants to be in personal fellowship with you. To do that, you must know Jesus Christ. His word tells us that no one can come to the Father except through Jesus Christ. That is His plan for all!

Day 1

A Beautiful Gift

Think about the most beautiful gift that you could possibly get. It could be big or small with lots of pretty soft, pink paper with little roses and lots of pink ribbons. That would be an exciting gift to get. However, suppose you never opened the gift? Suppose you sat it on a shelf and never bothered to see what was inside. Would you ever know what the box contained if you never opened the gift? God has a gift to give, and many times the gift is never opened. Many often say I'll get right tomorrow or I'll go to church or read my Bible when I get things right, and they never open the beautiful gift. The gift is always there, but it is never received with the love that it was given with.

God has such a beautiful plan for your life. It is more beautiful than you will ever realize. His plan involves the most beautiful gift that you could ever receive. This beautiful gift doesn't come in a big box with pretty paper and fancy ribbons. This gift comes from God in the form of the cross and a man named Jesus! You are so special to God that He gave His Son, Jesus Christ.

Our heavenly Father had such a perfect plan when He sent Jesus to be the Savior of the world. Jesus Christ is a magnificent and beautiful gift higher than any other. It will never grow old, lose its shine, or stop loving you. Jesus is the gift that brings salvation to the world. God gave sacrificially when He gave His only Son, so you could be forgiven. Jesus gave His life for you, so you could live life to the fullest. Have you opened your gift from God?

Go ahead and open the gift, go directly to the Bible, and read the word about His plan for salvation for you.

⁞⁞ Read and write John 3:16-17.

_____

_____

_____

_____

Those are some of the most familiar verses in the Bible. Chances are you could have learned verse 16 in Sunday school as a child. As you read verse 17, do you realize what it says for you and me? God sent His Son into the world not to condemn the world but to "save" the world- including you. God is not waiting to condemn you for all the wrongs you have done. He is waiting for you to come to Him and open the door. He is waiting to cleanse and wash you whiter than snow and forgive you of all of your sins. God gave His *One and Only* (1 John 4:9) as a sacrifice for you and me that would offer us the gift of salvation. Once again it is part of God's perfect plan for you. He loves His children (you) so much that He provided a plan for our salvation. God has a plan, not only for our lives here on earth, but for eternity.

Read and write John 14:6.

_____

_____

_____

_____

Jesus, Himself, reveals that He is the way to the Father. He knew the plan His Father has for Him, and He knows the truth. In order to know God, you must first know His truth and the way to go. Jesus is the truth and the life of God. There is no other plan available for salvation.

I pray that you realize that Jesus is the way to your Heavenly Father. Jesus is the gift that is available only if you receive Him into your life. This will be the greatest gift you have ever received.

Prayer Time

Dear Heavenly Father,

Thank you, Lord that you cared enough to send me the gift of Jesus Christ. Thank you, Lord that you have a plan of salvation to save the world. Thank you, Jesus that you were obedient in being the gift to save the world. Lord, help me to receive the gift and be changed at the very opening of the gift. I want the gift of Jesus Christ in my life. Help me to be changed and to have a new mindset. I realize that I do not have to be perfect to come to you, and I must be willing to receive from you. I realize that you will help me to change into the woman you desire me to be, in Jesus name. – Amen

Day 2

For All
Have Sinned

When the sacrifice of Jesus Christ is realized, often times feelings of unworthiness tends to rise up, feelings that may make think you are not good enough to receive "the gift," or that you are just too big of a sinner. God created you with emotions and feelings, and He knew that there would be times of trouble and sin in your life. There is not one that is without sin except for the Lord and Savior Jesus Christ. He is the only one that can offer up a clean sacrifice for you. Jesus is available to all and so is forgiveness if you will ask and receive.

Women are sometimes so hard on themselves by allowing feelings of guilt and condemnation to come upon them due to past sins, mistakes, or feelings. I've talked to women who feel like they have done some sin that no other has done. Women allow their emotions and thoughts to talk them right out of receiving the gift. I know I used to feel that way at times, and I'm sure many of you can relate. It is time to put a stop to following feelings and open the gift no matter what your faults or sins may be. *God shows no favoritism* (Romans 2:11). He does not love one of His daughters more than the other. He loves you all the same, and if you confess your sins and ask forgiveness, He will forgive you all the same. He loves you so much that no matter how you have sinned, His gift of salvation is free and available to you.

Read and write the verses about God's plan for salvation. Write the verses below.

1 John 1:9

Romans 6:23

Romans 3:23

All fall short of the glory of God daily. We all have our shortcomings, and are never without sin. One should always be conscious of the fact that mistakes are made and sins are committed. A Christian woman should be quick to repent and learn from her mistakes. One should never come to the point that she believes she has arrived and is without sin. Mistakes are not always bad because they will build and grow character. Often times when you are in the midst of a trial or situation, God is using that time for refinement to create in you a clean heart. He desires a relationship with you like none other you have ever experienced. As you grow and work through sin and temptation, your faith will emerge, and so will your relationship with your Daddy in Heaven! As a woman of God, you should grow daily and become more like Christ!

Are you ready to receive the gift of salvation? Maybe you have prayed and ask Jesus into your life before or maybe you never have. My prayer is that whatever point you are in your spiritual walk that you will receive the beautiful gift of Jesus Christ. This plan is for all and is needed for all to enter the kingdom of heaven. Jesus is waiting for you to open the door and welcome Him to come into your life.

:: Read and write Revelation 3:20.

This verse holds the key to it all. This verse says *that if anyone hears my voice and opens the door, **I will come*** (Rev. 3:20 paraphrased). It is up to you to turn the key and open the door!

The Bible has plenty of scriptures that will reveal the plan of salvation. God is all about love, and He cares for His children. His salvation plan has no flaws and no condemnation. The important fact is that you understand the plan in knowing that you must be involved in the plan. If you have never prayed and asked Jesus to live in you, it is time you do that now. He is standing at the door knocking and waiting for you to open the door to receive Him. The plan of salvation is the most beautiful gift from God, but it is at the will of the person to reach out and receive His gift. I have included a sinner's prayer for you to pray, and you will be eternally secure in Jesus. Pray this prayer aloud from your heart and you shall be saved. (There is something special about speaking it aloud and hearing it at the same time. There is power in your words.)

Salvation Prayer

Dear Lord Jesus,

I, _____, Come before you to ask forgiveness of my sins. I believe in Jesus, and I believe that He died on the cross for me and rose from the grave. I believe that it is God's plan for me to be saved and have eternal life. I believe that God loves me so much that He gave Jesus to save me. I, _____, give my life to you. Come into my heart and live in me. Change me and mold me into the woman you want me to be. I, _____, believe I am saved. Thank you, Jesus! – Amen

This is the greatest step you will ever take to becoming the woman God created you to be. If you just prayed that prayer for the first time, God is rejoicing with you. You are eternally secure, forgiven, and on your way to heaven. Please let someone in your church know that you prayed this prayer. Other Christians are there to encourage you and help you grow in your walk with the Lord. Share the good news of your salvation!

Day 3

There Is
Now No
Condemnation

I have good news for you today! You can have a healthy self-esteem in Jesus! Day-by-day you are building on the rock of Jesus Christ and moving to freedom in Him. You are on your way to being *Free to Be a Princess* that God has created. Today you are receiving freedom from condemnation! Women are the hardest on condemning themselves (Although men do it too!) and looking at our every flaw and mistake. The good news is that Jesus will never look at you the way you do! He sees you through His eyes, and His thoughts of you are so different from your own.

It is important to realize that, although, you will sin and mess up daily, there is no condemnation in Christ. Realize that when God brings forth correction and discipline, (and He will), it will be with love and compassion. His correction will build up and not tear down. Always remember, He is concerned with your well-being. The enemy is not. When the enemy tries to manipulate, control, or change you, it will be through condemnation and destruction. Always keep that bit of information on the forefront of your mind as you go through this self-esteem study. God is working to heal not destroy. When the words of condemnation come, take authority and speak against them.

:: Read and write Romans 8:1.

_____

_____

_____

_____

_____

Once you ask forgiveness for your sins, you are forgiven! God tells us in His word that He forgives us of our sins and washes us white as snow.

:: Read and write Psalms 103:10-12.

Verse 10

_____

_____

Verse 11

Verse 12

As His words states, "He does not treat us as our sins deserve." He does not treat us the way we do ourselves. His love is so great for you that the very second you ask for forgiveness, He forgives and casts it as far as the east is to the west not to be remembered again! It is you (and me) who will allow it to surface again and again. The sin gets relived over and over again in our minds, but not to God. You probably have sins and hurts that you have been holding onto for years. You may be dealing with a lot of guilt. You were forgiven by God, but you may have allowed condemnation to be a part of everyday life.

I encourage you to begin to make a choice to change your mindset today. You are free from condemnation! The good news is that God has forgiven you, and you do not have to live with a spirit of condemnation. You are on your way to total freedom in Him! Later in Step 4, we will deal with the mind and the battles of the mind, but for now just begin to make a choice to have a new mindset.

Prayer Time

Dear Heavenly Father,

Thank you, Lord, there is no condemnation that comes from you. Thank you, Lord, you are a forgiving God, and you love me enough to forgive me. Lord, please help me to be free from a spirit of condemnation. Help me, Lord, to watch how I condemn myself. I am your creation, and I am fearfully and wonderfully made. I am forgiven, in Jesus name. – Amen

Time to Journal

Take the time to Read Romans 7:15 through Romans 8:2. This is a struggle the Apostle Paul experienced. You will see transparency in this passage that Paul as a godly man struggled as well. In the journal area below, reflect on this passage and what it means to you. Make a list of things that you try to do, but later cause guilt and condemnation. Write your reflections below, and ask God for His help and His grace to strengthen you.

Day 4

Rejoice In Your
Salvation –
Your Gift!

Your gift of salvation is the greatest gift you will ever receive. There are no words to describe the amazing love that is held within our salvation. No human mind can comprehend the love that flows through the blood of Jesus Christ. His love for you is so great that He gave His, *One and Only,* Son just for you. What an awesome sacrifice He gave just for you!

∷ Read and write 1 John 4:9-10.

_____

_____

_____

_____

_____

God showed His love when He sent his Son as an atoning sacrifice for our sins. This is love, a love that we as His children can not fathom. It is the most precious love to receive. When He created this plan, He thought of you. This love is for all of His children, no matter whether one is male, female, black, white, tall, or skinny, He loves you!

I encourage you to rejoice in His great love. As a Christian, you have so much to be thankful for, so rejoice in Him. You have been purified through the blood of Jesus Christ. God is a mighty God, and He is all about love. His word tells you repeatedly about how much He loves and rejoices over you.

∷ Read and write Zephaniah 3:17.

_____

_____

_____

_____

_____

Wow! I just have to sit and read that verse time and time again because of the great love it speaks. God is mighty to save. He has a plan for your salvation. This is an awesome opportunity to open the door. Zephaniah the prophet speaks and gives a judgment call to repentance to a nation. He speaks of the day of the coming of the Lord. All throughout this book he refers to redemption, rejoicing, and restoration in Him. He does not want you to perish. He sent His one and only because He loves you so much. He takes delight in *you!* God is for you and not against you. He is waiting to quiet you with His love and draw you unto Him. What an amazing love it is that God even rejoices over you with singing. He is so ready to love and care for you, His child-His princess! All of your sins and everything you came to Him with doesn't change His love for you. He will never mention your past sins again. When you received your free gift of salvation, you were washed whiter than snow. He is ready to restore, heal, and move you forward in Him! The Amplified version of Zephaniah 3:17 says, *The Lord your God is in the midst of you, a Mighty One, a Savior, Who saves! He will rejoice over you with joy; He will rest [in silent satisfaction] and in His love, He will be silent and make no mention [of past sins, or even recall them]; He will exalt over you with singing.* What an amazing *love!*

Prayer Time

Dear Heavenly Father,

I thank you, Lord, for your amazing love. I can not comprehend it all, but I know that I am loved by you. Lord, I want you to be everything to me in my life. Thank you, Lord that I am your princess and that you take great delight in me. Thank you, Jesus; you are my King, in Jesus name. – Amen

Reflection

To those of you who know Him as your personal Savior, I urge you to stop and take the time to thank Him for your salvation. Thank Him for His grace and mercy that is new everyday. Sell out to Jesus 110%, and let Him change your life. Take the time to reflect on your walk with Him. In your humanness, there is always more to give to God, even when you think you are doing our best. Ask yourself a few questions about your walk. Here are few to get you started. (For those of you that are new in the Lord, I encourage you to think about these questions and maybe answer them in a way you desire to be in the future as you grow in the Lord.)

1. Do I know Jesus or just know about Him?

2. Am I sold out on Jesus, giving Him my all or just playing games?

3. Am I always requiring something of Him, or do I worship and praise Him?

Reflection

4. Is He my everything? What do I mean when I say He is my every-thing?

5. What does studying the plan of salvation reveal to me as a believer?

He wants to walk with you, talk with us and be a part of your life, but He can not if you will not let Him. Just like you desire relationships with people, He desires to fellowship with you. Invite him to become more involved in your life, and watch the change in you! Rejoice in who you are in Him and praise Him for your salvation. Everyday with Jesus gets sweeter. Your self-esteem is bound to be better.

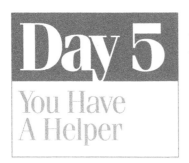

Day 5

You Have A Helper

In Christ, there is so much peace provided for you. God even provided a "helper" who will always be with you. The Holy Spirit will always lead you into a life of peace. In John chapter 14 starting in verse 16, Jesus tells about the "counselor" that will come and be with you forever. He, the Holy Spirit, will be the best counselor in the world. He will be your "helper" to help you make the right choices and guide you completely through life. The Holy Spirit will be there to cheer you on and encourage you. He will even correct you when you take the wrong path. God knew that you would need a helper, so He sent the Holy Spirit - the Spirit of truth. He will lead the way for you to live out your salvation!

The Holy Spirit will help you as well to have a healthy self-esteem. He will remind you of your preciousness to God and help you to realize who you are in Christ. Once again, open the gift and go to the Bible, so you may read His truth for yourself.

Read John 14:16-21, and reflect below what this passage means to you.

_____

_____

_____

_____

_____

The Holy Spirit directs you with love and truth as your counselor. Jesus said in verse 18, *I will not leave you as orphans.* He left the earth, but the Holy Spirit came to be with us, so we would not be alone. For those of you who may have been orphaned or feel like an orphan, this is good news to grasp. You are never alone and are never without love. I hope that you can come to see who He is through this study, so that you may know full well who you are because of Him. He is always with you, with your best interest at heart! I've often heard it stated many times that God writes the script, the Holy Spirit directs the play of our lives, and Jesus Christ is the superstar. You have a divine director leading the way for you!

▟▙ Read and write John 14: 26-27.

_____

_____

_____

_____

The Holy Spirit will also be your teacher, and He will teach you all things. He will remind you of who you are and what God says about you. You are fearfully and wonderfully made, and He will remind you of that. The Holy Spirit will also guide you into a new way of thinking, and you will be forever changed if you will listen and obey His teachings. The peace that He offers is far greater than anything you will find in the world. _He will lead you in a peace that surpasses all understanding_ (Philippians 4:7). He will not love you as the world has, He will never leave you or hurt you as the world has hurt many of you.

Do not be troubled and afraid, just begin to walk with and trust your new counselor and allow Him to create peace in your life like you have never known before. Allow the Holy Spirit to be your best friend and confidant. He can help you far better than any therapist, best friend in the world, your husband, or your parents. Seek His face and His peace! He will guide you to a healed self-esteem in Jesus name. You can have a healthy self-esteem because of Jesus Christ. You can be a woman that can look in the mirror and for the first time can see beauty like God sees. God wants you to change the way you see yourself and how you feel about you. Enjoy your journey to discovering _you!_

Read the passage in John 14:16-27 in its entirety and focus on your new counselor. Begin to talk with your counselor today.

Prayer Time

Dear Heavenly Father,

Thank you so much that you have provided me with a counselor. Thank you that He is always available and has my best interest in mind. Thank you, Jesus; you gave your life for me. Thank you for the peace that I can have in you, Lord. I need your peace and your guidance in my life. Please help me as I go through this study to receive the Holy Spirit as my helper. Help me, Lord, to learn to hear and listen to the Holy Spirit. Show me God who I am, in Jesus name. – Amen

Reflection

Moving forward as a Princess of God

I hope thus far you have begun to see your value and uniqueness that God has created within you. This step you have just completed is one of the most important of all. The sacrifice Jesus Christ gave for you is the best gift you could ever receive. When you accepted Jesus, you were washed in the blood and cleansed of all your sins. You were made new in *Him*. When Jesus went to the cross, He thought of you. He did not go to the cross for you to live a defeated life or have a low self-esteem. He desires for you to receive your healing, be healthy, and see yourself with new eyes! Without Jesus, you are incapable of knowing and seeing yourself differently. God desires to grow you up in Him. Accepting Jesus is the first step to a closer walk with God.

You may wonder what to do with yourself now that you have received Jesus. You may thinking about how do I "sell out" to God. Here are some suggestions to get you started.

1. Have a desire to change. Welcome the Holy Spirit into your life. There is nothing you can do on your own to make you any better. You need the Holy Spirit as your helper.

2. Get involved in a church that is teaching the truth of God's word. Get as much teaching and preaching as possible.

3. Begin to read and study the Bible. Hearing is one thing, but actually seeing and reading straight out of the Bible is another.

4. Pray! Prayer is talking to God and listening. It is two-way communication.

5. Get involved in a ministry group. Examples: Women Ministries, Bible studies, Sunday school, and others of interests.

6. Surround yourself with godly people. Talk with them and observe them. Also, get around them and listen. God gave us two ears so that we may do a lot of listening.

Reflection

7. Find a godly woman to mentor you. Watch and learn!

8. Do Bible studies and read books that will help you spiritually.

9. Be willing to repent and ask for forgiveness when you do mess up. Try to develop the fruits of the Spirit in your life (The Holy Spirit will help you).

10. Be bold! Be a woman after God's own heart! Be like King David; let the world know that you love God!

11. Be an imitator of God.

12. Love others and keep God's commandments

13. Praise Jesus everyday! No matter what the circumstance.

14. Meditate on His word, and hide His word in your heart. (Memorize scriptures so in time of need you can recall it.)

15. Be determined to give God your best.

Those are some suggestions to help you have a closer walk with God. The decision is yours to decide what you will do now. It is up to you to make the decision to sell out and draw closer to God. The Bible states, *"Come near to God and He will come near to you* (James 4:8a, NIV). You must always know that you are nothing within yourself, but if you will allow God to do His work, He will change you. The Bible says *I am the vine; you are the branches. If man remains in me and I in him, he will bear much fruit; apart from me you can do nothing* (John 15:5). You can do nothing without Christ! Remain in Him! He will take you to heights you never dreamed. You can be the woman in your dreams! You are valuable, and you are precious to God. You are His princess!

Step Three
Recognizing Your Self-Esteem

Get your mirror out and be ready to examine yourself. In this step, you will take a look into yourself to recognize your self-esteem. Do you have a healthy, damaged, or low self-esteem, or do you know? We always hear a lot of talk about self-esteem, and it gets blamed for a lot of issues. Do you realize your self-esteem could be the root of a lot of your problems? I had to realize that a lot of my hurts and pains came from my own self-esteem. Until I could see that my self-esteem was a problem for me, I really couldn't give it over to God because I was pointing the blame elsewhere. I couldn't be all God wanted me to be because I believed the lies of the enemy.

You already know that God created you good, and that He has a plan for your life. God's word tells you that *His promises are "yes" and "Amen"* (2 Cor. 1:20). *His word shall not come back void* (Is.55: 11). With knowing that God created us good and has a plan for our lives, you need to see where you are in believing that.

- Do you see yourself as valuable and beautiful? _____

- Do you really feel like a beautiful masterpiece? _____

- Are you angry with God or yourself over who you are?
  _____

- Do you like yourself? _____

- Are there others you are angry with? _____

- Do you even know where to begin to look into yourself and deal with your self-esteem? _____

These are a lot of questions that deserve some answers (Take time to honestly answer them if you have not already). I hope that this study will help you through the process of recognizing your self-esteem and allow God to begin to heal you. Remember, it is a process!

Thus far, you have been looking at who God your Father is and at the gift of your salvation that comes from Jesus Christ. Now, take a look at yourself to see who you really are. What do you see when you look in the mirror? Keep this question in the forefront of your mind as you begin to explore your self-esteem this week.

Right from the start, I would like for you to familiarize yourself with some common self-esteem terms. First, you are going to look at Webster's definitions of some terms about self. Since this is a book on self-esteem healing, I want you to know correct definitions so that you can look at yourself to see where you are. Begin to think of yourself in terms of these definitions and how each play into your life.

Definitions

1. **Self:** the total, essential or particular being of a person or individual.

2. **Self-esteem:** the satisfaction with one's self.

3. **Self-concept:** one's self-image.

4. **Self-image:** one's idea of one's self or one's status.

5. **Self-confidence:** the confidence in one's self and abilities.

Now that you are familiar with those definitions think of how they are all relevant to you, so you can move on to the next step. I would like for you to take the time to define each one based on you and why you feel the way you do. You may have several reasons, and some of them you may have to remember "why I feel this way". It could be painful, but let it all come out. You are on your way to healing. I have an example for you below.

Examples

1. **Self-confidence:** I am not capable of speaking in front of people. I don't feel that I speak clearly enough. (A Bible example is Moses.)

2. **Self-image:** I'm just a mother or a housewife. (Lots of examples in the Bible)

I have added some questions to get you started. Get a mirror and look yourself in the eye as you ask and answer the questions. You want to be realistic and honest with yourself. The visual view will help get you in touch with how you really feel. This is your opportunity to let it all out, and come clean before God. He knows it anyway; He just wants you to tell Him.

Self: Who are you?

_____

_____

_____

_____

Self-esteem: Why are you satisfied or not satisfied with yourself?

_____

_____

_____

_____

Self-concept: How do you see yourself as a woman?

_____

_____

_____

_____

Self-image: When you look in the mirror and see yourself, what is the first thing that comes to mind?

_____

_____

:: **Self-confidence:** How do you feel about your abilities?

_____

_____

_____

_____

You may not have an answer for all of these, but each of the questions will make you really stop and think about yourself. The whole point in doing this is to really make you do some heart searching. Take time to analyze your lives, feelings, and thoughts; try to discover the root of the issues with your self-esteem. Once you discover the root, you will know what to pray about. It is like in a garden; you must keep the weeds out or the bad stuff will soon over take it. When you clean up the garden you can cut the weeds down, but they return. It is not until you dig the roots of the weeds up that you gain victory over the garden. You are like God's garden, and He is working on you, for your good! He knows what is going on with you, but this is your time to release your self-esteem to Him. In yourself you can hide issues and ignore things, but they will eventually return unless you get to the root of the problem. Get to the roots and allow God to cultivate you with His love and grace.

All of us have a self-esteem, and it is the leading key to your self-image and self-confidence. Your self-esteem is truly how you feel about yourself, and if you do not feel positive for whatever reason, it affects everything about you. Women often fail to see themselves for who they truly are. In God's plan, you are a masterpiece, but you have to believe that you are significant in God's plan. Yes, I understand that we all come from different walks of life, and probably many of you have been dealt some pretty extreme circumstances that make you feel the way you do. Right now God is calling you to lay aside your past and come to Him. He wants to restore all that was lost and make you whole again. He can not do it if you are not willing to come to Him. I encourage you to just give God a chance. You may be thinking right now that you have issues that you can not understand why you had to go through them. Why did God allow this? Those questions are understandable, but the time has come to pray this prayer.

Dear Heavenly Father, I need you. I don't understand it all, but I need you. I am going to trust you. I've tried to do things my way, and "fix" my own self, but it hasn't *worked. I need to be restored because so far I haven't felt like a masterpiece. Your word says you have a plan for my life and that I am special to you. I want to trust you completely as I am changed by your truths of who I am, in Jesus name. Amen.*

Read and write Proverbs 3:5-6.

_____

_____

_____

_____

Read and write Hebrews 12:2.

_____

_____

_____

_____

It is not up to us to understand and know everything, but we are to set our hearts and our eyes on Him and keep focused. We are to acknowledge Him, and He will guide us in the right way. He will change the way we see or feel about ourselves. I believe one way to acknowledge Him is through this study. I believe that you are in this study by divine appointment, and He will guide you in His word to your self-esteem healing and freedom. Just as He led me to scriptures that brought freedom in my life, these same scriptures will bring healing into your life if you will trust and focus on Him. Focus on Jesus and trust in Him like never before.

Prayer Time

Dear Heavenly Father,

You know how I truly see myself. You know all my issues better that I know myself, and you are concerned. Although I do not understand my life, by choice today, I want to trust you with all my heart. I want to set my eyes on you so that I may be perfected in my faith, believing that you are healing me. I need your strength and grace as I walk through this process of self-esteem healing. I need you in Jesus name! – Amen

Day 2

Some Unlikely Women – Made Beautiful With Christ

Have you ever taken a look in the Bible at some of the women God used to do great things for Him? Many of the women in the Bible were not polished, perfect women, but yet God used them in beautiful ways. Let us think about Rahab for a moment. She was a prostitute. (You can read her story in Joshua chapter 2, Joshua 6:22-25, Hebrews 11:31, and James 2:25.) Rahab's self-esteem definitely needed a lot of healing. Rahab experienced a life changing event that totally changed her family tree. She opened the door and welcomed an opportunity into her life. Rahab became a part of the lineage of Jesus Christ. In Matthew 1:5, we read that Rahab was the mother of Boaz, who married Ruth and had Obed. Obed was the father of Jesse, who was the Father of King David and so forth. Read Matthew 1:5-16, and you arrive at Jacob, the father of Joseph, who married Mary, and they bore a son, Jesus Christ. God used Rahab in the family tree of Jesus. Was God concerned about her past? Certainly not! She was a changed woman. Rahab became a part of something beautiful that changed the world in spite of her past. Can you see yourself in this woman?

There are many other biblical examples of some unlikely women God had a big plan for. Read in Hosea 1-3 about the actions and love story between Hosea and Gomer.

Do you think Gomer had a self-esteem problem? Obviously she did because she was searching for love in all the wrong ways. Gomer could not seem to settle with a real love, but God continued to push Hosea to reach into the pit of her mess and love her anyway. God saw something different in her and gave her an open door, and He did it more than once. There must have been something special about her for God to take such an unlikely woman and write about her in the Bible. This descriptive love story between Gomer and Hosea is an example of the unending love Jesus has for you. Time and time again, He is willing to meet with you, pick you up, and completely restore you! This shows the grace and mercy of God and His unconditional love. Do you have anything in common with Gomer?

⠿ **Exercise**

Reflect on what speaks to you most about this portrait of love to an unlikely woman. What does it say to you as a woman?

_____

_____

_____

_____

Mary Magdalene became a devout follower of Jesus Christ. Before her following Jesus, she was possessed with seven demons (Luke 8:2). Mary Magdalene loved Jesus and helped Jesus in His ministry. John chapter 8:3-11 tells the story of the adulterous woman (some believe to be Mary Magdalene) who God used to show that He will not speak condemnation. Jesus showed this woman love regardless of her sins. Jesus did not condemn her. He told Mary Magdalene to *go and leave her life of sin* (v11). Can you relate to this woman?

You can also look at the life of the Samaritan woman Jesus met at the well. In John chapter 4, she meets Jesus at the well and has a conversation with Him. Jews and Samaritans don't associate with women like the woman at the well (John 4:9). Jesus was not concerned with that, He was concerned for her as a person. He spoke into her life, and He knew all about her life. He knew of her sins, but yet He shared with her about the living water, the living water that offers eternal life! God cares for us all no matter what!

Many of you may be dealing with a physical issue that affects your self-esteem. For this, you can look to the woman with the issue of blood for twelve years. (Mark 5:25-34). She had been under the care of doctors and was just getting worse, but when she heard about Jesus, she thought, "If I could just touch his clothes I will be healed". She was healed just by faith in that touch! Can you imagine her self-esteem for twelve years? Some of you can relate to her very well. God's word is real, and you can apply it to your life even today, right where you are.

⠿ Read Mark 5:34, and write the verse below.

_____

_____

_____

Jesus spoke and told her to go in peace. She was freed from her suffering because of her faith! He will do the same for you no matter what your need is. He will take care of it. He will heal your confidence, your self-image, and your total self-esteem no matter what the reason, past, or roots that caused it. He is a healing God that can heal mentally, spiritually, physically, and emotionally. Have the faith to just touch the hem of His garment and know that you shall be healed.

These women are just a few in the Bible that in our world today would seem very "unlikely" to accomplish something good for Jesus. No matter what you are faced with, you can look into God's word and find a woman that may fit your life. There may even be more than one that you can look to for hope. As you look at these examples of women in the Bible, reflect on the way that God changed them, healed them, and anointed them for His glory. By their anointing, they have done wonderful things that brought glory to the Father despite their past sins. He loved them just the same as He loves you. He is not concerned with your past mistakes. He is concerned with your heart. He is a God of restoration and healing. He will restore all that was lost. All of the women I referred to knew their past, but yet they moved forward. God revealed purpose to them. God knows all about you, and He is still has a purpose for you! Allow God to move you forward despite what you think may be a flaw, scar, or imperfection on you as a woman. God has such a perfect plan for your life. Allow Him to lead you to be a victorious woman who desires to be a woman after God.

Take the time to read the stories of the women mentioned. Search out a Bible example of a woman that relates to your life.

What causes you struggles, pain, guilt, or condemnation?

Prayer Time

Dear Heavenly Father,

Once again I come before you with my life. You know what is in me, and you know how it affects me today. Lord, help me to know your love like these unlikely women I read about. Lord, forgive me for my sins and help me Lord to move forward in your love and be forever changed like they were! I need your touch in my self-esteem today so that I may be healed and walk in peace, in Jesus name I pray. – Amen

Day 3

Princess - Be Encouraged!

You may feel like one of the "unlikely" women that you studied on Day 2, and just can not see what or why God would value you. Maybe you feel down in more than one area of your self-esteem. I encourage you to look into God's word, and let Him be the lifter of your head. It is possible that you have come this far in the study and can not believe that you are a princess of God. You can not fathom the concept of God's love enough to see how He could call you His princess. All throughout this study so far, we have read all about the love of God and how precious you are to Him. Now, it is time for you to be encouraged from right where you are. Oh, you may not see it or believe it, but there is healing in His word. He is working on you! He will heal every area of your life.

Take time today and reflect on the scriptures you have read thus far and be encouraged in His great love for you. God desires that you be encouraged by the reading of His word.

▚ Read and write Romans 8:17.

_____

_____

_____

_____

▚ Read and write out 1 John 3:1

_____

_____

_____

_____

Rejoice! You are a princess, and you are called a child of God! Those two verses you wrote above sum it all up. You are a princess, and you are loved. By God's grace, you share in the inheritance of Christ because you are called God's child. He has lavished His love on you and calls you His own. You are a princess through Christ! Now that you see that you are a princess, I want you to begin to act like one.

You may be thinking that you have never felt love must less to be "lavished with love". You may even think that you can not believe that you could truly be a princess in the eyes of God. God's word shouts throughout the scripture that you were bought with a great price, when Jesus gave His life on the cross. When you accepted Jesus Christ, He came to live in you. Your blood became the royal blood of Jesus Christ and all that is His belongs to you. You have an inheritance, princess!

As a child, you probably played dress up and wanted to be a princess at some point. The truth is when you accepted Jesus you became a princess of God. One that is greater than any appointed on the earth. I want to encourage you to begin to think and act like a princess of God. A princess of God is so set apart from the world's standards of a princess. With that in mind, I would like for you to compare the standards the world has for a princess versus what God would call His princess. Take time and gather your thoughts and answer the following questions. I have provided some cue words for you, but please feel free to compile your own list.

Cue words: Beauty, wealth, popularity, clothes, style, heir to the throne, royal bloodline

Write out below what you think a princess is?

_____

_____

_____

_____

_____

What makes her so special?

_____

_____

_____

_____

_____

Cue words: Her royal bloodline of Jesus Christ, Her heart, love, desire, love for self because of her Creator, inward beauty

:: Now write out below what God would consider a princess. What makes His princess special?

_____

_____

_____

_____

_____

Many times the enemy has so damaged your view of who you are that you only see what the world sees. Often the lies of the enemy are those that are so familiar to you that one can never believe or see the real truth. God's word is here to liberate you, and He is setting you free *verse by verse, line upon line* (Isaiah 28:10 paraphrased) as you go through this study into His word! As a woman of God, you are to set your heart and mind on things above, not on the things of this earth. What the world views as a healthy self-esteem and what God views are completely different. You are to have the mind of Christ concerning who you are and who you are to be. You are the princess God created you to be, not what the world or "society" dictates you to be.

:: Read and write Colossians 3:1-2.

_____

_____

_____

_____

My friend, you have been raised in Christ to a place that is above all the lies the enemy could convince you of. With Jesus Christ as your Savior, set your mind on things above as a princess to the *King.* Begin today to trust the ways of God by not leaning on your understanding, but leaning and trusting in Jesus, the *King.* Allow Jesus to *be* the King of your life and lead you in the way of becoming a free princess of God!

Prayer Time

Dear Heavenly Father,

Thank you that you see me as a special princess to you. Thank you, Jesus, for being the King of my life. Help me to be the princess that you desire. I will not live by what the world says. Help me Lord to set my mind on the things of you. I want to accept your love as you lavish it on me. I thank you that I am called a co-heir with Christ, and I love you for all that you have given to me. Allow me to begin to give back love to you by believing who I am in you, in Jesus name. – Amen

Day 4

Qualified To Be Free

Qualified? Are you qualified? In this day, you hear the word qualify many times and in various circumstances. Large companies want qualified people, and colleges want those that qualify for acceptance and scholarships. Real estate agents question potential clients quickly with "Are you prequalified?" I know in talking to many women, I have found that as a whole we will try to qualify ourselves. We question our abilities and talents wondering, am I really qualified to do this? Sometimes a woman will question whether she is qualified to serve God! Our world today sends us the message that if you don't qualify, then it is not going to happen. It is sort of a *Qualify or Else Theory.* Thank God that He has no prequalification! No matter who or what walk of life you come from, all you have to do is confess your sins, ask forgiveness, and accept Him as your Savior. No paperwork! You qualify! Praise God!

You have been qualified by Christ to share in the inheritance with God's holy people. You have an inheritance because of the King of Kings, Jesus Christ. God considers His children special, and you are a child of God. You are His princess! I want you to see the future that you have because you are in Christ. You are no longer who you used to be, and it is time to move forward in Christ. Hold your head up, smile big, and call yourself a precious child of God! It is vital to your self-esteem healing that you see how precious you are to God and the inheritance you have because of Christ. A princess walks with strength and dignity, and that is what God is calling you to do. To begin to see yourself differently, you must look at the change that took place when you gave your life to Christ. When you received Christ into your life, you received so much more than just your salvation. You received His love, His healing, and His restoration. You also received His victory, His forgiveness, and everything else you need to live in freedom. When you do not feel qualified it is easy to fail to realize the magnitude of the gift in your salvation. You accepted Christ as your Savior; now accept Him as your Healer. Let Him walk you into all that He has for you through Christ. He freely qualified you; now walk into your rightful place as a princess!

:: Read and write Colossians 1:12-13.

When Jesus Christ went to the cross, He did not go and sacrifice His life for you to live defeated and discouraged. He gave His life so that no one would perish, and you could live free! John 3:16 tells "the truth" about it all, but He goes one step further to say in John 3:17 that He came to save the world not to condemn the world! So many times a low self-esteem is led greatly by condemnation that He never intended for you to live with. He came into the world and went to the cross so that you could live free! Because of the cross, you are qualified and rescued from the darkness of the world. You are rescued from the evil tricks of condemnation by way of the cross. There is nothing that can stop the love God has for you. You are freely rescued from the darkness and by the blood of Jesus Christ; you are qualified to be free!

Remember back in Step 2 on Day 5 "More than a Conqueror", Romans 8:37-39 tells you that you can overcome. You are more than a conqueror in Him, and you can conquer your self-esteem issues or any others with Christ. You can overcome! You are accepted by God, plain and simple! No matter how many times you mess up and make mistakes (and you will) God still loves you. All of your past sins that the enemy tries to condemn you with can not stop God's love. Once you seek forgiveness, God casts it as far as the east is to the west! In other words, it will be remembered no more. You have been qualified to be *free!* God's grace and love is so much stronger than any lie, condemnation, temptation, or sin that the enemy could bring your way. God is a God of love who will take your mistakes and turn them around for His glory. God proclaims, He will never leave us nor forsake us, and that means even when you listen to the lies of the enemy, sin, or simply mess up, He loves you so much that nothing can separate His love from you.

Read and write Romans 8:28

No matter what comes your way, it will work for your good because of your love for God and His love for you. What a freedom revelation of His love! You are qualified by the blood of Jesus Christ to be free. I can not say it enough! You are being called out of living in the darkness of low self-esteem in Jesus name. You are being called to walk as a free princess of God and be more than a conqueror in Him!

Prayer Time

Dear Heavenly Father,

I thank you so much for the blood of Jesus that qualifies me to live a free life. Thank you that I do not have to live in the darkness of the world. Thank you that your love for me is so great that there is nothing that can separate your love from me. Help me to walk in your truths and love as my self-esteem is being healed. Thank you that because of you I am more than a conqueror. I can overcome in Jesus name. – Amen

Day 5

Free, Forgiven and Pure

Do you realize that you have been forgiven? Thus far, you have read the scriptures of salvation, forgiveness, and love, but have you applied them to your life yet? Do you realize all that Christ has freely offered to you? You are now alive in Christ! The old you has been made alive in Christ. Jesus has cancelled all of your sin and nailed them to the cross. Your past and old ways are forgiven, and you are new in Christ. If you are new, then why do you hold on to so much guilt and trash from your past? My question to you today is what have you not sought forgiveness on? Have you come clean with God and allowed Him to forgive you or are you still holding on to your little secrets? Allow me to encourage you today. God already knows all about your secrets.

He is waiting on you to confess them! Once again, it is all up to you as a woman to receive everything God has for you. When you confess your sins, there is freedom to have victory in that area. Will you give it all to Him, so you may be free, forgiven, and made pure?

:: Read and write Colossians 2:13-14

_____

_____

_____

_____

When you are forgiven, the sin that use to control you is nailed to the cross, thus setting you free. Are you free today?

What are you holding onto that would make you not feel like a princess? Are there any of these areas below that you need forgiveness. Are you ready to be free from the weight that you carry with them? Maybe there are others that are not listed that you need to deal with. (This doesn't have to be from your past. You could be facing it right now.) Circle all that apply and add others if needed.

guilt, condemnation	clothes	actions	abortion
weight	physical features	grudges	anger
bitterness	your home/car	past sexual sins	lies, deception
abuse	unforgiveness		

Figure 1

What is it for you? Make your own list here. Fill in the boxes below.

Figure 2

I hope that you will truly search your heart and get free of some things in your life that may have a hold on you. The freedom verse for this study is John 8:36: *So if the Son sets you free then you shall be free indeed!* I can not stress that verse enough. He is the only way to be completely free, but you have to be willing to surrender to Him. Seeking forgiveness from Jesus Christ and allowing Him to wash and cleanse you leads to a new life in Him. The blood of Jesus Christ can wash you whiter than snow and lead you to living a pure life before the King!

Read and write 2 Corinthians 5:21.

_____

_____

_____

_____

_____

Read and write Isaiah 1:18.

_____

_____

_____

_____

When I think of the word pure, the color white automatically comes to mind. I think of snow and white wedding gowns. The color is so calming and peaceful to me. When I think of the purity that Jesus Christ brings to my life, I am calmed and at peace with myself. Oh no, I don't deserve all that He has done for me, but He loved me so much that He desired to sacrifice for me, so that I could live in pure peace. He who had no sin and lived a righteous and pure life was sent to the cross for the sins of you and me. The blood of Jesus Christ will cleanse you whiter than snow. I encourage you to allow Him to purify and cleanse you. This is a cleansing process that may not be easy, but I can assure you it will greatly benefit you.

As you go through this process of self-esteem healing, I know there is so much to let go of and so much freedom that you can have in Him. Jesus Christ can cleanse you from the inside out. When you release yourself to Him, the miracle of freedom sweeps in like a big snow storm, and you are made whiter than snow. I encourage you to live in forgiveness, live free, and live pure. You are free indeed!

Prayer Time

Dear Heavenly Father,

I thank you Lord for the freedom I have in you. I thank you that your forgiveness is freely given and that the blood of Jesus Christ will cleanse me of all my sins and wash me whiter than snow. Thank you that because of Jesus Christ I am made pure, no matter what my past or my mind tells me. I am made alive and new in you, and I ask that you help me to walk into that freedom. I thank you for the blood of Jesus Christ in my life, in Jesus name. – Amen

This entire step has been about you recognizing your self-esteem and receiving encouragement for a healthy one. This step is designed to make you really examine you. It is like looking into a mirror to see what you really see. Not only has this step been about recognizing your self-esteem, but also to encourage you in Christ. Now that you see an area of need in your life that needs help, concentrate on what God's word says and be encouraged. From that, you can look at who God wants you to be in Christ and realize the areas in your self-esteem that really need restoration. God, your Father, wants you to bring it all to Him. Let Him began to heal and restore. You are precious in His sight, and you are a princess. It is time to start thinking like one!

Time to Journal

> But if we walk in the light, as he is in the light, we have fellowship with one another, and the blood of Jesus, his Son, purifies us from all sin.
>
> – 1 John 1:7

Write a letter to God to thank Him for the blood of Jesus Christ. Thank him for forgiveness and purity in Him. Take time to write about areas where you most struggle and ask for the blood of Jesus over that area! Allow Him to purify as you fellowship with Him today.

Dear God,

Love,
Your Princess

Self-Esteem Boosters

1. Be positive!
2. Think on good things!
3. Take the word "I can't" out of your vocabulary.
4. Speak life!
5. Be an encourager to others.
6. Receive a compliment with a simple "thank you".
7. Change your lipstick color.
8. Get a new hairstyle
9. Spend time with a girlfriend that encourages and uplifts you.
10. Take a walk and enjoy God's creation.
11. Look in the mirror and tell yourself that you are "fearfully and wonderfully made".
12. Make a list of your good qualities.
13. Stop thinking all about yourself and find someone else to show love and compassion to.
14. Start a good exercise program. (Exercise produces endorphins in your body and endorphins make you happy)
15. Place scriptures of encouragement around your house or office.
16. Fix yourself up daily - make-up, clothes etc. even if you are staying at home.
17. Smile on purpose!
18. Laugh at life!
19. Learn to do something new.
20. Talk to God and spend time growing closer to Him.

The key in boosting your self-esteem:

Remain in Me and I will remain in you. No branch can bear fruit by itself; it must remain in the vine. Neither can you bear fruit unless you remain in me.

– John 15:4

Step Four
Bust The Tape Recorder!

D o you ever feel as though you are walking around with a recorder in your head? Are you constantly replaying the same message over and over in your mind? Your mind is the biggest battlefield that you will have to overcome in dealing with your self-esteem. You may hear words of defeat, criticism, negativity, and other thoughts about yourself and areas of your life. It is like a big tape recorder in your mind, and every now and then, the enemy hit "play". You may replay words as far back as your childhood that caused you hurt, pain, or insecurity. There are words, comments, and junk you can not get past. I know you know what I am talking about. At one time or another, you have had to deal with it. It may not even be words. It could be feelings, thoughts, attitudes, or sins you committed. All this basically comes down to the term "bondage". You may not even recognize it as that, but it is bondage. Webster's dictionary defines bondage as "the condition of a slave and under subjection to a power, force, or influence". Wow! That really makes me stop to think. How about you?

Go with me as we continue the process for self-esteem healing and deal with the bondage of your mind. Are you a slave to your own mind? Are you ready to have a free mind?

> *Love the Lord your God with all your heart and with all your soul and with all your mind.*
>
> – Matthew 22:37

Step Four
Bust The Tape Recorder!

Day 1
You Have A Choice!

The time has now come that you recognize the power and force of the battle the enemy has launched in your mind and take authority over it! The tape recorder in our mind shall no longer hold you in bondage. Today, my dear sister, you are going to start *busting the tape recorder!* You have a choice as to what your mind is allowed to think. You shall not be a slave to the thoughts of your mind any longer. It is time to expose the enemy and his tricks. Maybe no one really knows all of the battles and struggles that you do have in your mind, but today is the day for exposure. It is time for a mind change and a new freedom in your mind and *life!*

To take authority over the enemy, you must stand on God's word to be equipped for the victory. You already know that you are more than a conqueror, and you can overcome the battles within your mind! You can do it! This was one of my biggest battles, but it has been one of my greatest victories! There is freedom! Trust me as you enter in to this next phase of the process.

:: Read and write Romans 12:2.

_____

_____

_____

_____

_____

:: Read and write John 8:36.

_____

_____

_____

_____

God's word is good news. You do not have to listen and conform any longer with what the enemy wants you to think and feel about yourself. Satan is a liar!

You have to make a choice today that you will no longer conform. You have to be bold and say "I will not conform to the world, and Satan I will not conform to your lies." You are not in bondage anymore of playing the games of the enemy in your mind. The Bible says that you are free! If you are in Christ, you are new and free!

Renew your mind! You have that choice. No one else controls your mind, but you. You can choose to fill your mind with God's word and believe His truth and be set free. If the Son, Jesus Christ, sets you free from the mind battle, then you are free indeed. This whole book is about being "free". You can not be free and have a healthy self-esteem if you do not control your mind. You have to bust the recorder! There is nobody in this world that can help you with your mind battles, but Jesus! Nobody can do for you what Jesus Christ can do, not your husband, mother, or girlfriends. There are no counselors, psychiatrists, or Pastors that can free you like Jesus. These people may give some aid or guidance, but they can not *free you!*

The lies of the enemy and the world would have you think that you have to live with it. You do not have to live with negative thinking, depression, guilt, condemnation, or anything else that is not of God because there is freedom. I encourage you to look to Jesus for your strength. Choose freedom today!

Prayer Time

Dear Heavenly Father,

I love you, Lord. I thank you that I am growing closer to you. I am beginning to see that you are the way to a healthy self-esteem, and that I can have one. Other things I have tried have not brought healing or filled the empty places. I pray for victory over the battle of my mind. I confess that I need you to strengthen me. I can not overcome alone. I make a choice today to begin to stand wholeheartedly on your word and trust you. Thank you for my freedom. Help me, Lord. I do not want to conform to the world. I can believe what your word says about me and live by your word. Bring scriptures to remembrance to help me overcome. In Jesus name, I choose you today. – Amen

Day 2
The Past Is The Past!

For many of you, the problems with your self-esteem come from situations in your past. There can be a powerful force of "bondage" over your mind due to your past. As we deal with this, I do not want to make light of your situations that you have faced in your life. Many of you have faced very serious and painful matters, and each needs to be handled with the proper care. This study is just the beginning of your self-esteem healing and the beginning of what God is going to heal and restore in you. However, I do encourage you to let God have His way and for you to begin to release your past. The past is your past, and the future holds a brighter day with Christ. Many times we relive our past daily in our minds and try to figure everything out. When one always thinks on the past, she misses the opportunities for the present day.

The enemy would like for you to live in your past and always feel defeated, but that is not what God wants for you. The enemy would like for you to dwell on your past continuously. Satan would love for you to think on your past mistakes, failures, relationships, struggles, and missed opportunities. The past is the past, and it is time to put it in the past and move forward in Jesus name. I am sure that some of you may say, "It is easier said than done", but I want you to realize that you are more than a conqueror in Christ. You can do it with Christ! Remember you have a helper- The Holy Spirit, who will lead the way.

Read and write Isaiah 43:18-19.

_____

_____

_____

_____

_____

God is doing a new thing in you, and you need to surrender your mind to Him. Welcome the change and the work of the Holy Spirit. God wants you to be victorious in your mind and to be free indeed. First of all, for God to do this process with your mind, you must admit that your mind is a battlefield. You must recognize that the tape recorder is there, and it does play those messages or send those negative feelings. Whatever causes you to feel down on yourself needs to be recognized. You need to call it for what it is and confront it. This will be hard, but it is possible! *All things are possible with God* (Mark 10:27). I had to work through several things, and you will too! Satan tried to get a new recorder in me even when I wrote this study. This study is directed by the Holy Spirit and not of me. I am His vessel that He is using! Satan has no authority, but he has tried every way possible to stop it with his ugly tactics, tricks, and thoughts. I refuse to listen to the enemy because I am equipped to stand on God's word. God opened my eyes to see all the freedom that is available in Christ. You too can be free from your past, your thoughts, and old self. It is time for a new way of thinking. You have to make a decision, with the help of the Holy Spirit, not to conform to your old ways of thinking any more. You are "free", and you are more than a conqueror in Christ, and it is time for a renewal!

Today's devotion has been short, but with good reason. I would like to encourage you to take extra time to pray today. I know the tricks of the enemy, and many of you are facing the hardest part of your freedom in your self-esteem. Many women have told me that this step is one of the hardest to deal with, but yet brings the most victory. I know that it was for me. You have to expose and face the roots of the battle in your mind, and that can be very hard. The enemy is a liar, and he doesn't want you to be free. Spend time praying, so that as you expose the enemy and his lies and tricks in your mind, you will be ready for battle.

Daily, I have included prayers for you. I encourage you to take your prayers to another level. Give God everything! Let Him help you as you go through busting the tape recorder and allow Him to comfort and strengthen you. He will hear your cry, and He will be faithful to carry you through. It is sometimes helpful to write down your prayers. At times this is comforting for me because I can focus and let it all come out. Later, I can go back and read my prayers and see how God has answered them. Call it a faith builder if you will! Be encouraged today, and spend time in prayer talking and listening to your Heavenly Father.

Prayer Time

Dear Heavenly Father,

I pray as I begin to bust the tape recorder that you will help me to deal with all that I am facing. You know everything about me, and I need you to carry me through. I want to forget the former things and focus on the new. I know that you are doing a new thing in me, and I want all the restoration and healing that you have for me in Jesus name! Help me, Lord, to grasp hold to your truth and freedom. Open my eyes to see what has caused the battle in my mind and why I allow it to hold me in bondage. I know I am more than a conqueror, and I am ready to be renewed, in Jesus name! – Amen

Day 3
Where Are Your Thoughts Coming From?

> *...Take captive every thought to make it obedient to Christ.*
>
> – 2 Corinthians 10:5

Where are your thoughts coming from? That is a big question that you must ask and answer for every thought that you allow to enter your mind. As you go through life, your mind can either be positive or negative. It can either produce good thoughts or bad ones. The choice is up to you! What are you allowing your mind to think? I would like to challenge you to examine where your thoughts come from.

Ask yourself a few questions about where your thoughts are coming from. Create a checklist in your mind to evaluate every thought. Here are some questions for your checklist below:

- Is this thought speaking love or condemnation?

- Is this thought good for me or destructive?

- Is this thought coming from heaven or hell?

- Is this thought obedient to Christ?

(You can also change your checklist from examining your thoughts, to attitudes, words, feelings, and so forth.)

If the answer to your questions above is condemnation, destructive, and coming from hell, you need to dismiss the thoughts. Every wrong thought that doesn't line up with the Word of God, must be brought into obedience. *Change your thinking and give the devil no foothold* (Ephesians 4:27) in your mind. When you give the enemy one thought, he will take two or three more to go with it. I am sure you have heard the old saying "you give someone an inch, and they will take a mile". The enemy is a master deceiver (but he has already been defeated) at trying to take what is not his and then some. First Peter 5:8 tells us that *Your enemy, the devil, prowls around like a roaring lion looking for someone to devour.* The enemy is looking and waiting for you to give him an opportunity to get his foot in the door. He will lie and bring confusion into your mind if you allow him. *The devil is a liar, and he is the Father of lies* (John 8:44).

The word will help you identify where your thoughts come from. Now, you must decide what you need to do with it. If it is speaking condemnation and destruction, begin to speak the word of God over it. Take authority over that thought. Tell the devil that you are a child of God. You are a princess, and you will not fall into his trap. Tell him to leave your mind alone!

When the enemy says you are a nobody, you are just a Mom (for all of you stay-at-home Moms), or you will never amount to anything, bring those thoughts into obedience. When he tries to tell you that you are a failure at being a Christian or say you can never be what God expects, press stop on the tape recorder! The enemy is a liar. These lies create the battle in your mind. Those thoughts are not from God and have no place in your mind. As a child of God, you have authority in Jesus name to conqueror those thoughts. It is all up to you to stand equipped for the battle and take authority. I could write a whole new study dealing with the authority that you have in Jesus name to overcome.

▪▪ Read and write 1 John 4:4.

_____

_____

_____

_____

_____

Jesus overcame for you, and you have Jesus in you, so that makes you an over-comer too! *He has given us the physical and mental strength, and ability over all the power that the enemy has* (Paraphrased, Luke 10:19, AMP). My dear sister you have authority and power because of Who lives in you. You even have the mental strength to stand against the enemy. Exercise your power and authority that you have in Jesus. Begin asking for the Lord to strengthen you and lead you so that you can be ready for the battle. Ask Jesus for help with the battle in your mind.

You must also realize that God has given you a sound mind, He has made you a conqueror, and you are a winner of the battle in your mind.

▪▪ Read and write 2 Timothy 1:7.

_____

_____

_____

_____

_____

Step Four
Bust The Tape Recorder!

God has not given you a spirit of fear. He has given you the power and authority to stand up to whatever is holding you back. It may be fear of rejection, memories, hurt, pain, abuse, and struggles that keep you from living a free life.

Read and write John 14:13-14.

_____

_____

_____

_____

Realize you are not alone in the battle. The Lord is with you through every battle, including the ones in your mind. You can ask for freedom in Jesus name. You can ask for a sound mind and anything else you need, and He will do it.

You have to be equipped and ready for battle, so you will know how to fight back and *win!* Nothing is impossible with God. If you have self-esteem issues that come from bondages in your mind, then this is just for you. You have power and authority over the thoughts that enter your mind. The victory of the battle in your mind belongs to you!

Prayer Time

Dear Heavenly Father,

I surrender my mind to you. I give you authority over my mind! Guide me, Lord, in taking every thought captive and obedient unto you. Thank you that greater is He that is in me that he that is in the world. Thank you that I do not have to live with a spirit of fear over my past because I am forgiven in you. Create in me a renewed mind and set me free, in Jesus name. – Amen

Day 4
Breakthrough of the Mind

For as he thinks in his heart, so is he...

– Proverbs 23:7

Have you ever just stopped to think about some of the thoughts that get in your head about you? Sometimes you can wake up in the morning with negative thoughts in your head about yourself, and these thoughts can affect the rest of your day. If you continue to dwell on the thought, then it's easy to fall in self condemnation. Then you find the tape recorder playing all day. God's word tells you in Romans 8:1, *that there is no condemnation for those who are in Christ Jesus.* I have heard women speak condemnation over themselves continuously. No one else has to do it for you. If you are not careful, you will condemn yourself more than anybody else.

I know many of you deal with serious issues in your minds. It is up to you to control what goes on in your mind. No matter what lies come to your mind, you are special. You are a child of God, and you are a princess! What thoughts are entering your mind about you? What comes to mind first in the morning or at the first glance in the mirror? Are you taking your thoughts captive? You will be what your mind tells you to be.

Be careful what you think and allow to enter into your mind. God gave you a good mind to be used for good things and good thoughts. Remember you are an overcomer, so think like one. Let us take a look and answer some questions as to what you are allowing in to your mind.

1. What are you watching on TV? Too much television and watching inappropriate material can invade your thought life.

2. What kind of books are you reading? Steamy romance novels and horror stories allow thoughts to enter your mind that are wasteful. If you are going to read, find a book that is edifying and is a benefit to you.

3. Who are you talking to and what are you talking about? If you are talking to someone, make sure that person can lift you up. Be careful who you let influence you and what you allow to pass through your ears!

4. What else are you allowing to invade your mind? You must ask yourself are all of these TV shows, books, and other things obedient to Christ. If not, begin to fill your mind with new material.

I can not stress the importance enough of taking control over your thought life. Don't be afraid to stand up to the enemy (and your own mind) and take authority. If you think you are a failure or less than, then it is hard to be an overcomer. You have to think you are a winner, act like a winner and talk like a winner to be one! You have the power because of who lives in you. You are a winner because Jesus lives within you. You are important, and God has purpose for you.

God knew that all of us would have issues and face tough times. He clearly tells us in His word that we can all bring our cares and our anxieties to Him, and He will care for us. As you prepare to journey through this day, immerse yourself in His word. Meditate on the scriptures and the truth that He provides for you. God has a plan for your freedom victory. Breakthrough is coming your way!

Read and write 1 Peter 5:7.

_____

_____

_____

_____

Working it all out!

Part of busting the tape recorder will require you to work though some "stuff" or "junk" that may be buried deep and long forgotten. The enemy knows just the right time for you to hit "play" on your recorder, and then you are off and running with condemnation and negative thoughts.

It's important not to skip this part. This is a vital part of the process. Remember you are busting the recorder! This is crucial to you becoming a free woman with a healthy self-esteem.

Exercise

Take out a journal or a piece of paper and begin to write every message, comment, feeling, or negative thought you have ever had about you. These messages could have been spoken by a parent, friend, husband, and so on. These thoughts could be from your own condemnation about you. Take your time and really meditate on the replays you hear over and over. Let yourself go as far back as you can remember in your life. This is an important part in your healing process. I urge you to seriously meditate as much as possible. Once you remember it and surrender it to the Lord to be remembered no more, then your freedom will come.

⠿ Read the examples of a few messages women often deal with in their mind.

1. You will never be anything.

2. You can not do anything.

3. You always mess things up.

4. I am ugly.

5. I am _____ (what do you think about yourself?)

6. I see this flaw.

7. You are a _____. Can not you do anything right?

⠿ Think about some feelings you have, and then answer the questions below.

1. Do you have feelings of inferiority as a woman?

2. Do you feel second-rate?

3. Do you have issues about your weight?

4. What about past relationships?

5. How you deal with things?

I am sure there are many other issues that you deal with in your mind. These are just a few popular ones with women. As you complete your assignment above, lay the sheet of paper aside because you will come back to it.

Give it all up!

Now that you have faced the issues, do not be concerned about the size of your list (I hope that you let all of your issues surface). If you are in this study with any kind of self-esteem issue or past struggle your list should be long. Don't be embarrassed by the size of your list that you bring before God. My list was really long!

> *Catch for us the foxes, the little foxes that ruin the vineyard...*
>
> – Song of Solomon 2:15

I wanted to make sure that I left nothing uncovered and revealed it all. I wanted freedom, and I was determined. You may think it's small or insignificant, but nothing is too small for God. If it's a big deal to you, it's a big deal to God! Little thoughts grow into big thoughts, and if it is not obedient to Christ, then deal with it **today!**

▪▪ Read and write Philippians 4:6-7. Take the time to read this aloud and listen to yourself while reading.

▪▪ Read and write Psalms 55:22.

His word plainly tells you to cast all your cares on Him because He cares for you. His word also tells you not to be anxious about anything. Present your request to God and you will be given a peace that we can not began to comprehend. This is what God's love does for you. He is the peacemaker. He will sustain you as you go through tough times, and He will never let the righteous fall. He will help you to guard your heart and mind.

Go back to your list of messages you wrote earlier. It is time to take the thoughts captive unto Him and bring them into obedience. Hold the list out in front of you. I want you to look at it real hard, and then out loud tell God you are giving it to Him. Hold your paper up in the air and surrender. Say, "I am *free* in Jesus name! I am no longer a slave to my own mind!" John 8:36 says that *you are free indeed*.

Give it all to Him! Surrender it all never to pick it up again. Think on these thoughts no more! It can no longer be used against you. Put God's word into action. I encourage you to hold your list out and pray the prayer below.

Dear Heavenly Father,

Here is my mess, my battle in my mind. I have no desire for these thoughts. I wrote it all down and allowed it to surface so that I may cast it all on you. You know everything that I have brought before you. Your word tells me that you are concerned and that you will never let the righteous fall. I pray for breakthrough in this area of my life today. I know that I am more than a conqueror, and I can be free from the bondage of my mind. I know that I can not do this by myself, only you can set me free. Give me the strength and the peace that I need to have a victorious mind in Jesus name. I am free from these thoughts that have so wounded my self-esteem, in Jesus name. – Amen

Ladies, the tape recorder just got **busted!** Now take your list and tear it to shreds. You are free indeed! No more bondage of the mind. Rejoice in the Lord!

▪▪ Read and write Philippians 4:4.

_____

_____

_____

_____

He wants you to be at peace with yourself today. As you walk with Christ and grow in His knowledge, you will be changed. You are even expected to be different. Once you have come to know that you can have peace with a renewed mind, and then you have a weapon against the enemy. God's word tells you that your peace is in Him, and you are to live in accordance with the Spirit. Take a deep breath and rest in your new peace of a renewed mind. You are one step closer to a healed self-esteem in Jesus name.

Prayer Time

Dear Heavenly Father,

Thank you Lord for the healing process you are leading me through. Thank you Lord that I can cast all my cares on you. Help me Lord to change the focus of my thoughts. Help me to have a complete breakthrough in my mind. Help me Lord with the battle and teach me to rejoice in you. In Jesus name. – Amen

Step Four
Bust The Tape Recorder!

Day 5

Seek Peace

I hope that yesterday on Day 4 you received breakthrough in the area of mind battles. I hope you smashed your "tape recorder" real hard! It would probably do some of you good just to walk outside and yell at the enemy "I am free!" I am free in Jesus name! Wow, wouldn't that feel great? Maybe jump a few times as if you were smashing the recorder under your feet. Go ahead and put your foot on the head of the enemy and destroy the thoughts once and for all.

I want to, once again, encourage you in your journey of self-esteem healing. I encourage you as a princess of God to seek peace! As His princess, peace in Him belongs to you. He is the peacemaker and you know Him, so peace belongs to you. In Day 4, you emptied out some "junk" in your mind, so go after His peace today to fill your mind. Seek peace daily and live in peace!

:: Read Romans 8:5-9, and write out Romans 8:6 below.

_____

_____

_____

_____

This passage is describing two mind-sets in which one leads to death and the other to peace. This is a perfect example of the mind being a battlefield. There is a constant battle going on between your fleshly desires and the spirit. If you follow your mind, you are walking in the flesh. Walking in the flesh feeds the sinful nature that is within you. Sin is what will lead you to bondage, and that is unacceptable. Sin will lead to death. I told you to be careful about what you allow in your mind!

I referred in an earlier step to an example in Romans 7:15 through Romans 8:2. There is a perfect example of trying to do the right thing, but you do the other. All of you have been there at one time or another. The struggle over sin does not make us less than or a failure. Every human being is faced with the struggle of sins. People are given choices to make everyday as to which way they will walk.

Romans 8:6 says, *The mind controlled by the spirit is life and peace.* I chose life and peace. How about you? The choice is up to you, but it clearly reveals the best choice in the Word. You can walk in the spirit and have peace. Do not let your mind overrule and say "I just can not do it". In one way that is true. You can not do it alone, but He that is in you will be your Helper. Therefore, you can do it. God will give you the grace you need to walk in the spirit and have a life of peace.

As I have stated time and time again, this study has equipped you with a lot of scripture to stand on when the battle begins to rage. When the mind battle starts, just stop and meditate on God's word. You can control your thoughts with the leading of the Holy Spirit. You can have perfect peace in your mind.

Read and write Isaiah 26:3.

_____

_____

_____

_____

Don't let your mind rule! Keep in perfect peace! You can have perfect peace when you keep your mind on Him. When you are thinking on Him and filling your mind with the word, there is not much room for the devil to get a foothold. The Amplified version reads as follows: *You will guard him and keep him in perfect and constant peace whose mind [both its inclination and character] is stayed on You, because he commits himself to You, leans on You and hopes confidently in You* (Isaiah 26:3). When you lean on Christ and hope in Him, there is peace. When you set your mind and even your character on Him you will have perfect and constant peace. What a promise! God will give you the grace to pursue peace. The Bible tells us in 1 Peter 3:11, To seek peace and pursue it. Begin to seek peace today and pursue it with perseverance.

Read and write Psalms 34:14.

_____

_____

_____

_____

Step Four
Bust The Tape Recorder!

It is declared in the Old and New Testament that we are to seek peace and pursue it. Take time to read Psalms 34. It speaks so much encouragement to seek the Lord, and those who take refuge in Him are blessed. Those that look to Him, their faces shall be radiant, and He will hear your cry. Not one of you shall be condemned by Him. He has heard your cry of a broken heart and low self-esteem. He is healing and restoring you even now. Seek His peace!

As you studied in previous steps, you know that as a Christian, the Holy Spirit lives within you. You have so much power and authority in Christ. All you have to do is exercise the power to be free in Christ. Your mind does not have to be filled with negative thoughts replayed over and over, nor does your mind need constant reminders of comments and mistakes from your past. The Holy Spirit resides within you and because of Him, you can have constant peace. The Holy Spirit will help you to be positive, but He will not help you be negative. In other words, He will give you the grace you need to be positive. My prayer for you is that you will receive what you have read and surrender the battle in your mind to the Holy Spirit and live free.

Prayer Time

Read this prayer and fill your name in the blanks.

Dear Heavenly Father,

Your word tells me that I, _____, can cast all my anxiety on you. I come before you now in prayer giving you the issues of things I have been dealing with about myself. Some of them are replayed messages or feelings that I deal with. Many of them I have lived with for a long time and the pain that goes along with them. I no longer chose to listen to the enemy any longer. I, _____, stand on your word and ask that you set me free in my mind from this moment on. Set me free from the tactics the enemy has used against me and held my mind in bondage. I, _____, trust in you and need you to carry me. I ask that you let your peace take the place of all that has kept me in bondage. Help me to set my mind steadfast on You, so that I may have perfect peace in You, in Jesus name I pray. – Amen

The Reward

TOGT

> *Now the Lord is the Spirit, and where the Spirit is there is freedom.*
>
> – 2 Corinthians 3:17

You are probably wondering what "TOGT" means, and so did I when I first read it. My Pastor would write notes and sign it at the bottom "TOGT." It really makes one stop and think for a moment, but when you realize what it stands for it is contagious. The Bible tells us in Philippians 4:8 that we are to *think on good things*. That is what my Pastor's "TOGT" reminded me to do. I am thankful that my Pastor allowed God to use him in that small way to remind me of what I am to think about. Try the Pastor's TOGT; I promise it's contagious!

Earlier in this step, you busted the tape recorder in your mind. Now you need to fill it with new things. You have cleaned out some old bondage "junk", and now there is room for the good stuff. Fill it with what God's word has for you to think.

Read Philippians 4:8, and write the verse below:

_____

_____

_____

_____

Go back and circle or highlight all the things that you are to think.

Philippians 4:8 sums up what we should think. If you think on these things, you will also speak and act on them too. By applying His word to your words and thoughts, it will change your attitude. Thinking on good things is what changes mindsets and the way one feels about life. God wants to radically change you to become the woman of God He planned

The Reward

you to be. He wants all of you which include your thoughts (mind), tongue, eyes, ears, and heart. He is moving you forward with an ultimate goal in mind, and that is to be like Christ. Will you ever be perfect? No, not on this earth, but you will become more like Christ the more you grow in Him. Will this make you prideful and arrogant to have a healthy self-esteem? Certainly not! Through this process you are becoming more like Christ. You are coming humbly before Him to see who you are in Him.

There is less of me now, and so much more of Him in me! – Anonymous

He has a plan for you. Remember you are His masterpiece! Princess, I encourage you to pursue peace. Have peace in your mind in Jesus name. Walk in peace, think peace, and speak peace daily. You will have total peace!

Princess, the tape recorder has been busted! You are free indeed!

Step Five
The Process of Freedom!

Let's take a minute to recap what God has accomplished thus far. Have you surrendered it all to Him?

1. You know that you were created by God, and you are a beautiful masterpiece.

2. You are fearfully and wonderfully made.

3. You know that Jesus is the way, the truth, and the life; and He came to set you free.

4. You have searched within yourself to see who you are. You have searched to recognize your self-esteem. You are a real princess of God!

5. You have busted the tape recorder that controls your mind, and replays things that you don't need to hear.

I pray in Jesus name that you have worked through the previous lessons, and surrendered to God to allow Him to do His work in you. Self-esteem is a building process of healing. Your self-esteem issues did not happen over night, and it is a process in opening up areas for healing as we build a totally healthy and healed self-esteem in Jesus name!

Just as you lay a foundation to build a home your self-esteem must have a solid foundation of knowing who your Creator is. The foundation to a healthy self-esteem is on the Rock, Jesus Christ! On that Rock, Jesus will take one issue at a time and heal the areas of need and promote you to a new level of self-worth, confidence, and image to create a healthy, healed self-esteem. It is a work in progress, and it requires a process you must go through to reach the next level of self-esteem victory. With every victory in your self-esteem other things will arise that you probably never realized was a self-esteem issue! The more you deal with and surrender to Jesus, the more freedom comes into your life. In this step, you are going to go one step further in the process. Let's get to work.

Step Five
The Process of Freedom!

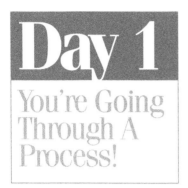

Day 1

You're Going Through A Process!

For *you* are God's workmanship. You are His handiwork, and He is pleased with you! He created you, and He likes what He creates! He created, fashioned, and formed you on the potter's wheel exactly the way He desired! You have already touched on this subject some in step one. You already know that you are created in His image, and He called His creation very good and that includes you. You must realize that God created you "very good" and He created you to do "good works". He created you to be a good wife, a good mother, a good friend, and everything else you need to be. What He desires you to be is "good". You are not good of your own self. Because of He who lives in you, you are capable of good works. *You are to have no confidence in your flesh* (Philippians 3:3), but have total confidence in who you are through Christ. That scripture sets you free from trying to "be" so much on your own. You are His masterpiece that He created; allow Him to work through you! God has already prepared the way in advance for you to do well, so just surrender and allow Him to lead, instead of you.

:: Read and write Ephesians 2: 8-10.

_____

_____

_____

_____

_____

Right from the start, God says in this verse, that "For it is by grace that you have been saved through faith. You have been saved by an unmerited love that can not be explained or understood in our human minds. Grace is a gift from God. See how important you are to Him that He has gifts for you! He has the gift of grace which you can only receive by faith in Jesus Christ. There is nothing you can do to earn this gift! It is not a competition, beauty pageant, or contest to see who can be the best to get the most from Him; it is freely given by faith in Him. There is no work that you can do on earth to earn His love and grace!! It is freely given.

The verse goes on to say, *For we are God's workmanship* – You are a work of art.

You are His masterpiece. You were created by His hands. Since you are a masterpiece, He wants you to feel like a masterpiece through Christ. He wants all of your emotions, thoughts, and everything about you to come in line with what He created you to be. Does this mean we will be perfect? Absolutely not! *There is no one righteous* (Romans 3:10). Jesus Christ is the only perfect one. If you are in Christ, then you can be changed to be more like Him. We don't have to "do well" on our own. Get in alignment with the word and "be good" because of Him that lives within you. If one continually tries to always do well, it will never happen. You are a human being. You have a flesh that is capable of sin! Know that God has already prepared you in advance to do good works, but first you have to "be" the person God desires and out of that person good works will flow. God is not as concerned about your doing as He is the "being". I heard a saying once that was somewhat like this: "If we will spend more time focusing on being what God created us to be instead of finding ways to do things to make us look and feel better and earn acceptance and love, then our Spirit will become stronger than our flesh and lead us into doing good." In the midst of our being in right relationship and standing with Jesus Christ, good works will naturally flow. He created His masterpiece to do well, so focus on being, and the doing part will come naturally by His grace and love.

▪▪ Read and write Romans 7:24-Romans 8:2.

_____

_____

_____

_____

_____

I love what the Apostle Paul wrote in Romans 7:24. He says, *What a wretched man I am!* Let us look at it a little differently. "What a wretched woman I am!" I am capable of sin although I want to do good sin is in me, and I need to realize that. That should free some of you by just reading that the Apostle Paul faced his struggles with sin, but yet he wrote the majority of the New Testament. Obviously, Paul recognized His weakness, his capability to sin no matter how hard he tried. However, Paul also realized that through the grace of Jesus Christ, there is no condemnation. He is free and forgiven because of grace! He can be who God created him to be, and so can you. You can be a mighty woman of God with a healthy self-esteem. Everything is in Him. You are His Masterpiece created to do well! You are beautiful, and if you will allow Him to be in you, the good will flow!

⠙ Read and write 2 Corinthians 5:17.

_____

_____

_____

_____

_____

When you became united in Christ, everything about you changed whether you realize it or not. When you accepted Jesus, it is as though you were stripped of your old self. Daily you must die to self to put the old behind you, and stop hanging on to the old you. You are a new creation in Christ and the old is gone, including a low (poor) self-esteem. God wants to radically change your self-esteem and all the other things to do with your "self". He wants you to be transformed into the woman He designed you to be. It is like when you get in the shower, you daily wash off the old. You get out of the shower feeling new and refreshed. The same is true in the spiritual. You shower daily, so you are a new creature! In Christ, there is a new you!

Remember, that God created you, and you are good! Princess, you are fearfully and wonderfully made! In Ephesians 2:10, you see that you are God's workmanship, His beautiful work of art. He has a master plan for you. It is time for you to shower off the old you, and allow God to shower you with His newness.

Prayer Time

Dear Heavenly Father,

I thank you that I am made new in you. Thank you, Lord that you created me as your masterpiece. Forgive me, Lord, for not always seeing myself as your masterpiece. Thank you for my salvation and that I am new because of the blood of Jesus Christ. Strengthen and encourage my self-esteem as I go through this process. Help me, Lord, to see what you see. Open my eyes and my heart to see your truth, in Jesus name – Amen

What if God kept a record of our sins? That would not be good! Praise God that He is a merciful God and forgives His children. God first forgave you of your sins, and He expects you to forgive others. His word tells you that you are to forgive just as He forgave you. What if He were like us sometimes? People in general hold on to some ugly feelings of hurt, pain, and frustration. Then it turns into a grudge to resentment to bitterness to hate and discontent. People tend to keep records of wrong doings and other failures and never reach the point of forgiveness toward others. If you are not careful, all of those ugly feelings caused by unforgiveness can take root in your own hearts even as a child of God. You have to guard yourselves and be careful. You have to check yourself and make sure you are forgiving just as Christ forgave you. You can not be the woman of God you were created to be when you are holding on to unforgiveness. It is time for a forgiveness check within you. You may already have some of those feelings hidden deep down inside that cause some of the way you feel about yourself. Is this correct? Search within yourself so that you can come clean with God.

Webster's dictionary defines forgiveness as an "excuse for a fault or offense or to renounce anger or resentment against." Keep this definition in mind as you go to the Bible to seek the scriptures on forgiveness. As you go to God's word to read scriptures on forgiveness, take the time to really meditate on His word. Try to plug your name in His word, and see how it opens your eyes and heart to what forgiveness truly is.

Read Psalm 130:1-4 and write verses 3 and 4.

Verse 3

_____

_____

_____

_____

_____

Verse 4

_____

:: Read and write Mark 11:25.

:: Read and write Colossians 3:13.

It is so important that you examine your heart and be on guard as to what is held in your hearts. It is imperative that you try to live with a clean heart. Before moving on, please stop and ask God for forgiveness on anything you have been letting stew in you. Ask Him to reveal these things to you. Ask Him to wash you clean of those ugly feelings. It could be painful, but sometimes healing can be painful. Just remember you are going through a process!

:: Read and write Proverbs 4:23.

Step Five
The Process of Freedom!

_____

As you end the day, ask God to help you to have a clean heart. I encourage you to allow the Holy Spirit to minister to you and lead you. Listen to the still small voice within and be obedient. He will reveal the areas where you need to allow forgiveness to flow. Flow in forgiveness, and be free indeed!

Prayer Time

Dear Heavenly Father,

Forgive me, Lord! I come before you asking and seeking your forgiveness for _____. I know that there are areas that I need to surrender to you and allow your cleansing flow to take place. I need your forgiveness and grace to move forward. Thank you that you first forgave me and you do not hold it against me. Help me, Lord, to set people free in your name. Create in me a clean heart that harbors no unforgiveness, in Jesus name. – Amen

Day 3

Showers of
Forgiveness
and Love

Praise the Lord for His love for you and me. Praise the Lord that He forgives all sins, and He abounds in love. He is slow to anger, and He does not harbor His anger forever. In other words, God does not hold grudges. He has compassion on us, even when one fails. As a godly woman and a new creature, you must strive to be like Him. You can not do it alone, but with the help of the Holy Spirit all things are possible.

Maybe there are areas in your self-esteem that are a product of the action of others. There may be some of you that have experienced terrible abuse either mental and emotional or physical abuse. Forgiveness may be hard for you to do. It could be rape, terrible childhood memories, divorce, a broken heart, shame brought on by another, or just the pain of the hurt of your past. The list could go on into issues that trouble the lives of women (and men alike). There is so much freedom in forgiveness when you allow God to take over and begin to walk you through forgiveness. You can, with God's help, forgive those that have hurt you. You can experience a freedom shower through forgiving others. You may be thinking right now that you don't want to or you really don't harbor any unforgiveness or do you? I encourage you to ask God to search your heart and begin to show what you are holding onto. You may be thinking I don't want to confront the issue and face the person. Know that you do not have to face the person in order to forgive them. If God desires for you to confront the issue and the person, He will give you the grace and strength to face it in His timing! Healing through forgiveness is possible with God. Forgiveness is a choice. You can either choose to hold onto hurts and the past, or you can choose to take a freedom shower.

I am sure that many of you may have a lot of deep rooted issues that need to be forgiven. I know how much power this one area had in my life when I surrendered it and faced forgiving others. I got a freedom shower of grace and love to forgive, and He will do the same for you! God can help you through it. Give Him the freedom to show you the unforgiveness you are holding on to. Be willing to let it go when He reveals it to you.

⸭ Read Psalms 103:1-13, and write verses 3, 8, and 9 below.

Verse 3

Verse 8

Verse 9

Time to Journal

In His great love for us, there is grace, mercy, and love freely given. Are you willing to accept the freedom that He has for you, or do you desire to hold onto your junk? Many times we are often comfortable with our junk although it may be damaging us. God is offering a free shower in Him today. Are you willing to let Him wash and cleanse your life, your pasts, your thoughts, your mindsets, your hang-ups? Self-esteem healing requires that you surrender your "junk" to Him and let Him work you through the process of renewal and restoration. He can not renew what you are not willing to give Him!

In order for you to be radically changed, you have to set some things free.

Exercise

Get a blank sheet of paper. Write the title, "Forgiveness" at the top of the sheet. You will then need to make a list of the names of people that have caused you pain or hurt and have brought damage to the way you feel about you. This may hurt to think about, but it is a step you must take to open the door to freedom in this area. The hurt may be big or small.

In the step before, you were dealing with the action, the words, and now you are dealing with where they came from. So, make your list. Take your time to complete this list. After you have finished making your list, put it aside because you will need it later. It may take several days for you to create this list, allow yourself time to think about it.

> So if the Son sets you free, then you shall be free indeed.
>
> – John 8:36
>
> This truth is yours so be free!

Prayer Time

Dear Heavenly Father,

Lead me in forgiveness. Help me, Lord, to forget all the negative things that I have harbored so long and the people that caused them. Help me to forgive like you forgive. I know that in myself I am not capable, but with the help of the Holy Spirit I can forgive. Help me to live free from holding to old hurts of others that are not pleasing to you. I want to be free. Help me to for give those that have hurt me, in Jesus name. – Amen

When I sat and made my list, I thought of many people that said or did things to me that affected how I felt about myself. I thought of people as far back as my days in middle school, and many others who came later in life. As I made my list, there were lots of tears and even a little bit of laughter as reality set in. Some things I just couldn't believe that people had said and to think that I let it affect me. Others things hurt to remember. Many times I'd wonder "why" they would even do what they did. The list was really long, and some things were trivial and others were serious, but to me they all had been recorded to my tape recorder. They were there to rise up at the worst of times and to alter the way I saw myself. This is how the enemy works. He can take the smallest comment and turn it into the biggest issue that we as women may hold onto for the rest of our lives!

As God and I talked about this list, He revealed something so beautiful to me. He told me what I needed to do to move forward and be healed in His name. It was a soft whisper in my heart that brought tears to my eyes. God said, "Now forgive them". God told me to forgive them, every one of them, and then forget about it. He told me to forgive all the people that had ever hurt me in any way. Did that feel good? No way! I felt like some of them need to come and ask me for forgiveness and apologize for the junk they said. However, I love a God that first loved me even as a sinner. He forgave me even when I didn't deserve it. There is no choice in the matter! My God knows what is best for me, and He knows how to restore and heal me. God is concerned with my every need and feeling I have. He definitely wants me to feel good about myself, and I must obey because He knows what He is doing. I am called to be a forgiver. This was a breakthrough, and it will be for you too!

As I cried over my list, God began to reveal something else that was even more precious than the first. As we go through life, we often look at who said or did or caused things to happen in us, and point the finger here and there. We fail to realize that we do some things too that can cause a low self-esteem. All of my actions, words, sin, and everything else that I have done and feel terrible about was brought to mind. Many times the enemy will try to remind me of "junk" just to pull me down. I know that I have been forgiven, but yet I allowed it to frustrate me. God was definitely revealing to me through His word that I was forgiven. He had forgiven me long ago, but I was still holding on to it. God spoke to me, and said, "Now forgive you"! When He spoke that to me, there was immediate freedom. I became free indeed! For years I had felt guilty, but this time I forgave myself!

What I failed to realize was that God had forgiven me and forgot it all the day I asked, but I held onto it. I thought about it, dwelled on it, and did just what the enemy wanted. He wanted me to think I was bad, but not anymore. I was free in Christ! As long as the enemy could keep that stinking thinking in my mind, I would never rise up to be the woman God created me to be. I would always hold myself back. Nobody else would have to do it. I would keep myself from moving forward. Oh, what healing God can give you if you will just open up and receive it! He loves you so much. He gave His only Son just for you to be free! He'll do you just like He did me, if you will just allow it. Your testimony may not be the same as mine, but it'll be your healing, your freedom, and your deliverance!

Read and write Psalms 40:1-3.

_____

_____

_____

_____

God will not hear your compliant, but he will hear your cry of brokenness, shame, disgust, and hurt. He will put a new song in your mouth. He will show you who you are in Him. You are valuable to Him, and you are His masterpiece! He will change the way you look at you. He desires to do that for you!

Exercise

Go back to Psalms 40:1-3 that you wrote above. In the verse above, circle all the words that refer to you – I, me, and my. Say the verse aloud and put your name in it every time you come to a circled word. Underline all the action words that He did. Write all that He did for you in that one verse. List all the action words below.

Example: He turned me around.

_____

_____

_____

Time to Journal

Now, it is your turn!

Go to your journal or get a blank sheet of paper. At the top of your paper write "All about *me*". Make a list of your actions, words, bad deeds, whatever you have done that may have brought the low self-esteem. This part is all about you. You need to take the time to deal with *"you"*. Deal with whatever is pulling you down. It is time to be free. You shall not live in defeat anymore!! You may want to refer back to *Recognizing your Self-esteem* and read some of what you wrote.

He has set your feet on solid ground and gave you a firm place to stand in Him. The Lord has just heard your cry and knows your pain. He will restore, heal, and fill you with joy. He will put a new song in your mouth. He will help you to see differently. He will help you to forgive yourself. Give Him the glory for lifting you up and turning your life around.

Getting free!

Take your "Forgiveness" and "All about me" lists and hold it out in front of you and give it to God. Pray the prayer on the next page as you give the list to God.

Take your lists and tear it to shreds. You are free!! I think it is time to put your lists in the trash or whatever method of disposal you like! Take time to write and reflect on how you feel about this process. Then take time to read Romans 8 on your own. (Read about 8 verses at a time, so you can meditate on them as you go).

Dear Heavenly Father,
I thank you for this process. Lord, it hasn't been easy to do this, but it wasn't easy when you hung on a cross for me. You did it with me in mind. I thank you that you are lifting me up and healing me. I know that I am your daughter, and you care about my every need. You know the people that have hurt me even more than me. I realize that the time has come for me to forgive and let go. Now, I give them up to you. I forgive these people as your word says I should. I know that this is my choice, and I chose to

Time to Journal

forgive them and release them to you. I forgive them in Jesus name. I lay this list at your feet and ask for your strength to walk away from it. I know that I can not do this alone, but I am more than a conqueror with you. I also realize that I need to forgive myself. I have made mistakes and messes. I have done things that I am not pleased with, but I know that you have forgiven me. I thank you for forgiving me, and I know that I must now forgive myself. As I walk through life, I realize I will make mistakes, but I also realize that your grace and mercy are new everyday. I believe that I can do all things through Christ, and I chose to forgive myself. I forgive myself in Jesus name. I am free! Thank you for leading me. I ask that you help me to be the woman, the masterpiece, you created me to be, in Jesus name. –Amen

Prayer Time

Dear Heavenly Father,

Thank you for the freedom that I have in you. Thank you for opening my eyes and my heart to see the truth about forgiveness. Thank you that I can forgive myself because you have forgiven me. I pray that you will strengthen me to stand firm in forgiveness when the negative thoughts try to come against me. I need your strength, grace, and love to walk the righteous path and live a victorious life. Thank you, Father, for loving me enough to reach down and pick me up out of the mud and mire and set my feet on solid ground, in Jesus name. – Amen

Day 5

Armed For Freedom!

You have come so far in leaving your old junk behind and rising up to be new. In the days to come, I know that you are going to walk as a victorious woman. As you continue, even after this study, you will need to be fully prepared to walk as God created you to walk. The beauty of Christ is that He doesn't just take you through a process and leave you there. He guides, teaches, and leads the way for you. He writes in His word exactly what you need to do to be a victorious woman of God. He has a plan for you in His word about every aspect of your life, and how to deal with it.

Read Ephesians 6:10-18. Write verses 13-17 below.

Verse 13

_____

_____

_____

_____

Verse 14

_____

_____

_____

_____

Verse 15

_____

_____

_____

_____

Verse 16

_____

_____

_____

_____

Verse 17

_____

_____

_____

_____

In God's word, He tells us of the schemes of the devil. John 16:33 tells you that *you will face trouble in this world, but God has a written plan in His word just for those times.* When the devil is trying to work his way into your thoughts and your emotions, you need to be ready. Never let your guard down! Be ready to stand firm, and face the devil with truth. When the enemy comes to attack your self-esteem and confidence, put the devil in his place. You must be ready every day. You must "put on" the full armor of God, and when the flaming arrows come, you can put them out with truth. Use the truth from His word to fight the battle. I hope that you have some Word deep in your Spirit from the scriptures in this study that have equipped you to fight. I hope you are armed for freedom! No longer can you allow the enemy to get into your mind, your attitude, your self-esteem. You have to be ready for the battle and spiritually dressed for it. Always be alert and watching for the enemy's attacks on your self-esteem. Stop the tricks of the devil with the armor of God. Give the enemy no place to start and keep pressing on in the full armor, claiming your victory!

This sounds very easy to do and so spiritual. I can assure you that when the enemy attacks, it may not feel so great. He will do whatever he can to attack your self-esteem, so take heed to the warning. Just know that you are more than a conqueror with Jesus Christ. The devil lost the battle a long time ago. You can win with Jesus!

Prayer Time

Dear Heavenly Father,

I thank you that I have armor to stand with. Thank you that you thought ahead and knew that I would face troubles and need the armor to fight with. Thank you for your truth and your word. Help me to always recall your word and be able to withstand the tricks of the enemy. I thank you so much for your freedom, love, and grace. Thank you that you have set me free, in Jesus name! – Amen

Reflection

This has probably been a difficult step for you. I would like for you to reflect on what all this has meant to you below.

What has helped you grow the most? What scriptures have spoken the most to you? This is a time for you to reflect your true feelings.

Step Six
Free To Be!

My friend, my sister in Christ, you have come so far in this study of self-esteem healing. I have to believe that at this point your Father in Heaven has started such a healing in you that you can not walk away from it. I pray that you praise God for the restoration and healing that He has poured into your self-esteem. As you enter in to the finale' of this study, I want you to reflect on your progress. I know that you have made some! I know that your self-esteem is not the same anymore because I know that God is changing *you* from the inside out!

God's word tells us in Isaiah 55:11 that *His word shall not come back void.* There will be a return on the word that you have read during this study. You will be changed simply because of the word you have read. The degree of change depends on your willingness to surrender to the Holy Spirit and allow Him to refine you in the healing process. Refinement is the process that we sometimes don't like, but it is best for us. God will always refine in love and never in condemnation. He will pour out His grace to help you be everything that He desires you to *be!*

As you enter in to this final phase of *Free to Be a Princess*, I want you to search your heart. Ask yourself a few questions:

- Just how free am I?

- Am I really free to be what God desires me to be?

- Have I surrendered it all to Him?

- Am I sold out on Him?

Ask God to help you answer these questions because no one can answer them for you. When you determine in your heart that you want to be free with Christ, it is then that your freedom will burst through like the new morning sun. When it comes, you will know it!

Day 1

Truth Of
The Word

The Bible is the word of God that has stood the test of time, and it has been passed down through generations. The Bible is inspired of the Holy Spirit and is useful to all who read and live by its words. He purposed for His word to guide us into his divine plan for our lives with instructions. I encourage you to get in His word to seek God and His plan for your life.

The Bible is brought to life by the Son of God, Jesus Christ. In the Bible, you will see that the Word became flesh. The Word became flesh for you. The word is Jesus! I encourage you to get to know the Jesus! Many people read the word, but do not know how to apply the word of God to their lives. I have heard it said before. "It would be better to read the Bible once and know it than to read it fifteen times and never know truth and apply to our lives." It's not beneficial to your life to say I did my Bible reading for the day and not leave with biblical truths that you can practically apply to your life. As a Christian and a godly woman, I am required to go to another level in reading the word. I have to seek Him through the word and be changed by it so that I may be a witness for him and allow the word to cultivate newness in my life.

Does your life exemplify someone who knows the word and lives by it? You can look at the fruit of your life and inspect it to see how you are doing. What if we all took the word as truth and lived by it, and truly lived a free victorious life? How awesome that would be? The Bible covers everything you and I will ever need about every situation we will face. God has an answer in His word. It doesn't matter if you can not recite the books of the Bible; the question is do you know what the word says and can you apply it to your life? God wants you to live by His word. Jesus is the word, and you can get closer to Jesus by reading His word.

Let's go to the scriptures to read how the scriptures came into existence.

Read and write John 1:1-4.

_____

_____

_____

_____

██ Read and write John 1:14.

The word is God! Thank God the Word became flesh for us! The Word was with God, and the Word was God from the very beginning. The Word became flesh as the Father's only begotten Son and made His dwelling among us. He has brought us grace and truth. The Word is God, and the Word is **truth!** Jesus went to the cross for you so that you could be made whole. The word (Jesus) became flesh. He was sent to heal and set you free.

I encourage you to grasp a hold of what you read. The Word is not a lie; it is the only truth. God does not lie; Satan is the Father of lies. God's word is love. When you spend time in the word of God, everything in your life will change. Isaiah 26:3 *says you will keep in perfect peace him whose mind is steadfast in keeping your mind on Him and His word, you will have perfect peace.* Abiding in His word brings peace. He is the Word and you are to abide in Him.

██ Read and write John 15:5. (Read all of John chapter 15:1-17)

██ Read and write 2 Timothy 3:16.

Read Psalms 119:9-16, and write below what this passage is speaking to you.

_____

_____

_____

_____

_____

Remain in Him, and He will lead you in the way that you should go. *Jesus is the way, the truth, and the life* (John14:6). He will teach, guide, train, and even correct you with His word. Hide His word in your heart so that you do not sin. Allow God's word to fill your heart and mind so that you can live a life pleasing to God. You must realize that apart from Him, you can do nothing. You will never live a life of peace, be free from the slavery of your mind, or walk victorious without Him. You simply will never be all that God purposed you to be without Jesus.

You are probably thinking, "How do I do this?" All throughout this study you have been in His word. It is time for you to stay and abide in His word. Allow it to take root in your heart, so it will be there forever. His word tells you to remain in me, and I will remain in you (John15:4). It is time for you to make a commitment and determine that you will give God your all. Now that you know what God's word says about you, it is time for you to take your place.

You read earlier in lesson five about putting on the full Amour of God and being ready for battle. The word of God is your sword, but if you never read the word, you'll never get your freedom! You have to get in the Word, know the Word, and let the Word get into your heart. It is one thing to call the devil a liar, but when you know God's word says, in John 8:44 that *he is the Father of lies*, then that is when you get bold and remind the devil who you are! When the word of God is coming forth in you, there the spirit rises up to settle the issue. You are a child of God, you are co-heirs with Jesus, and He has set you free. In God's word is the very presence of God, verse by verse. The scriptures talk about your self-esteem, healing, and freedom. Some of those scriptures are found in this study, but take time to search His word. He will show you everything you need. Live by His word, and hide it in your heart, so that you can live free!

Prayer Time

Dear Heavenly Father,

Thank you for your written word. Thank you that the word became flesh in Jesus Christ, and I can get to know you better through your word. Create in me a desire to know your word and to crave the very essence of it. Help me to be able to apply it to my life so that my life can be productive. Lead me; guide me, so I may produce good fruit. Thank you for leading me to victory in my self-esteem. Thank you that when you died on the cross you thought of me, in Jesus name. – Amen

Day 2

Take Off Your
Grave Clothes!

God wants so much for you to be changed and to walk victoriously, but it is time you come forth. Rise up and walk! You have read many scriptures that have encouraged your healing process, but you now face a pivotal point in your self-esteem. Will you let go of the past and your old way of thinking? Let's go straight to the word before I go any further, this part is good.

Read John 11:38-44. Just stop and read it a few times and then read it aloud so you can really get the word in your heart.

Verse 40

_____

_____

_____

_____

_____

Verse 43

_____

_____

_____

_____

_____

I love what Jesus had to say here. *Did I not tell you that if you believed, you would see the glory of God* (John 11:40). He speaks very straight forward just like a parent speaks to a child, "Did I not tell You?" Well, yes indeed He did tell you. All throughout His word, God tells you about who you are and how special you are. However, the question you must ask yourself is, "What do I believe?" Do you believe you are new in Christ?

John 11: 43 is awesome in power because Jesus tells, *Lazarus, come out!* Out Lazarus came! Lazarus didn't chose to stay in the grave because he was just made new! The grave is in the past, and Lazarus chose to obey and rise up and come forth just like Jesus said. What does that tell you to do?

It is time for you to rise up and come out of the past. You are a new creature in Christ, and you have a great opportunity right now to be free of your past. The choice is yours to stay in the grave of a low self-esteem or rise up as Christ calls for you to come forth out of your grave. The grave offers stinking thinking, bad attitudes, hurt, guilt, anger, bitterness, unforgiveness, and more. There in the grave is a low self-esteem, poor self-image, no confidence, feelings of no self-worth, and total unhappiness within you.

My dear sister, if you will just rise up with Christ, oh what joy you will have! He is calling you to come forth out of "your grave". He is calling you to come forth and believe His word. He is calling you to rise up out of your mess and come forth in Jesus to be victorious!

Jesus is calling you to take off your grave clothes. Take off your bondage, chains, "junk", and all that is holding you back, and *let it go!* You are being called to come forth in Jesus name, to be the princess of God you were created to be. You no longer need to wear your grave clothes of the past. If Lazarus didn't take off his grave clothes, what would his life would be like?

This whole passage is just so awesome when you realize the power in coming forth when Jesus calls. The Bible tells us to believe, but often we fail to believe and fail to allow God to do His work in us. Don't hold onto your grave clothes any longer. God has forgiven you, and it is time to change.

:: Are you ready to let the old go?

:: Are you ready to rise up out of the grave?

:: Are you ready to replace the grave clothes with new joy and peace?

:: Are you ready to smile at who you are when you look in the mirror?

Believe in His word. He sent the word to heal you.

What else do you need to let go of? What is keeping you in the grave of low self-esteem: sin, unforgiveness, guilt, shame, addictions, disobedience, weight, your finances, your clothes, physical attributes, character issues, mind battles? What is it for *you?*

So often we become comfortable with our stuff, thinking that it is easier to hold onto and wear the problem daily than it is to let it go. Lazarus could have said, "No Jesus I think I like these grave clothes, this smelly hole that I am in. I think I'll just stay here." Think of the appearance Lazarus would have if he chose to keep his grave clothes. What is your appearance like? Are you portraying peace,

joy, happiness, contentment, or are you in a battle of living a lie, low self-worth, sadness, and misery.

Read and write Psalms 139:23-24.

_____

_____

_____

_____

_____

I encourage you to take the time to meet with God and ask Him to search your heart. Ask Him to test you and show you where you stand. Ask Him to show you what stands in your way of being free to become the woman of God He purposed you to be. Ask him to show you the grave clothes that need to come off. Ask him to search you of things that you are still holding on to that you need to be free from. You already know that you were created _fearfully and wonderfully made._ From the beginning of time, God had a plan for you. Receive all that He has for you today!

God's word states that you can be a child of God and co-heirs with Christ. When your mind is on Him, you will have constant, perfect peace. His word also tells you that because the Son set you free, then you are indeed free! The truth of the matter is that God's word is real, and His word is for you.

Time to Journal

"Take off the grave clothes and let them go!"

Pray about whatever is holding you back from rising up with Christ and admit it!

Figuratively speaking, what grave clothes do you need to take off? Write them below.

Prayer Time

Dear Heavenly Father,

Thank you for calling me out of the grave of low self-esteem. Thank you for showing me all that I am to you. Thank you that I belong to you. Please reveal to me any grave clothes in my life that I am still trying to hold onto. Search me, O God, and know me. Show me what I need to see. Guide me through the process of restoration and help me to walk and choose life over the grave. I want to be free in you, and I surrender to you. Heal me, Lord, in Jesus name! – Amen.

Day 3

Dress To Be
A Princess
Of God!

Now that you are rising up to take your place and you have taken off the grave clothes, it is time for a new wardrobe! I know you like new clothes. It is time that you get properly dressed to be the masterpiece God created you to be. By God's grace and mercy, you are given a new royal wardrobe to wear. As a woman who is made in the image of God you need to rise to your appointment. Rise up and dress yourself, and walk as a princess of God. Get into agreement with what His word says about how He created you, and walk victoriously though life.

Let's go search God's word so you may receive complete freedom to be the princess God has called you to be.

▪▪ Go and revisit 2 Corinthians 5:17-21. Focus on verse 17 and write it below.

_____

_____

_____

_____

Stop and reread this verse a few times. Read it at least nine or 10 times if you have to until you get what His word says to you. Sister, if you are in Christ, you are a new creature. The old has gone!

▪▪ Look at the end of that verse, and write those words in big bold letters below.

_____

_____

_____

_____

Here are different Bible translations of the end of 2 Corinthians 5:17.

▪▪ The NIV- ...the new has come!

:: The KJV- ...behold, all things are become new.

:: The Amplified-...Behold, the fresh and new has come!

The end of verse 17 speaks of what has taken place in your self-esteem. God has done (and is still doing) a healing work in you. You have been made new through Christ. I'll go one step further and tell you that there is even newness and freshness about your relationship with God. From this day forward, you will never be the same. Thank you Jesus! Rejoice in your newness! The new has come. Everything before you is fresh and new, and Christ has made the way for your freedom. All you have to do is receive His word, stand on it and walk in His truth. Receive His word today. You are *new!*

:: Read and write Mathew 9:16-17.

Jesus is offering you a spiritual freshness. The newness that Jesus is bringing forth in your life can not be held to the ways of the "old" you. Your old self-esteem is no more! You are a new creature in Christ, and He is pouring into you such a refreshing wine that you will not be able to contain. You can not be half-hearted or double-minded. You must come to the decision to lay your life down, and allow Christ to do His will in your life. You can not try to patch this, fix this, or cover up this or that. It simply will not work. You must come clean and sell out to God, so that He can heal and restore all the broken, brittle, and weak areas within your self-esteem. You have to give God 110% of who you are. Jesus is offering you a new life by faith in Him, and you must trust Him.

You, my dear sister, are a new creation. You are no longer who you used to be. God took the initiative to offer you a plan that would bring restoration and fulfillment in your life. Jesus Christ came and through Him all things were made new and restored. You can not restore you. Your counselor, your best friend nor your husband can restore you. They just don't have the plan. Jesus Christ is the only one that can heal you and fill all of your emptiness you have inside. You are new in Christ, and He will fill you with new wine, in a new wineskin, that you have never experienced. You will not be able to contain all that He has for you.

As a new creature in Christ, a princess of God, you must dress with a wardrobe of royalty. You are provided a royal bloodline through the blood of Jesus Christ, and you must carry yourself as a woman of strength and dignity. You are somebody. You are beautiful. You are a masterpiece.

The Amplified Bible reads, *To grant [**consolation and joy**] to those who mourn in Zion, to give them an ornament- a garland or diadem- of beauty instead of ashes, the oil of joy for mourning, the garment [**expressive**] of praise instead of heavy, burdened and failing spirit; that they may be called oaks of righteousness [**lofty, strong and magnificent, distinguished for uprightness, justice and right standing with God**], the planting of the Lord, that He may be glorified* (Isaiah 61:3).

Reread all the bolded words above. That is your new dress code as a princess of God.

The very day you received your salvation, you were bestowed a crown of beauty. You were filled with the oil of gladness and given a garment of praise instead of the failing spirit of despair. You became somebody in Christ! You are free to be the princess God created you to be!

A garment as you and I know it is just a piece of clothing, but this garment that the word refers to is special. Stop for a moment and think of your garment of praise, victory, and beauty to be in your new wardrobe. Add on preciousness, confidence, love, and value as accessories to make it complete. Then you can show world your new wardrobe of self-worth, acceptance, honor, joy, and trust. Dress your mind in good thoughts, a Christ-like attitude, and peace. Wrap yourself up in Christ. I mean literally put it on and wear it. Go to the mirror and say, "I choose to wear all that Christ has for me!" A piece of clothing represents nothing for you until you put it on. When you put on the garment (clothing), you will feel and see the benefits of the garment. You know what it feels like when you put on a new dress or piece of jewelry. So go ahead, and accept your garment from Jesus Christ. ***Put it on!*** This garment will be a reflection of the outer and inner being. It is now up to you to put it on and wear your garment as a princess would her royal ball gown and her tiara. Hold your head up high and smile. Realize that you are somebody in Christ. It is your choice to receive this very day from God.

You have so much in Christ that makes you precious in His sight. You are made in the image of God. God does not intend for you to feel like a failure, down on yourself or living in the past, He has something beautiful to offer you, and it is free! I pray that you will receive what Christ offers in every aspect of your life mentally, emotionally, physically, and most importantly spiritually.

Read and meditate on the verse below.

You shall also be [so beautiful and prosperous as to be thought of as] a crown of glory and honor in the hand of the Lord, and a royal diadem [exceedingly beautiful] in the hand of your God.

— Isaiah 62:3, The Amplified Bible.

You are so precious to God that Jesus shares His glory with you and sees you as exceedingly beautiful. God created you to be "very good", the best, and nothing less will do. He looks beyond your flaws, scars, and all your imperfections that you can come up with, and He sees a beautiful woman of God that He adores! You are His daughter, His princess!

Walk in joy, for the joy of the Lord is your strength.

— Nehemiah 8:10b

Now that you are dressed to be a princess, you must act like one. As a woman of God, you are special to your heavenly Father. You must come to know that truth in your heart. You will never find another love and relationship like the one you can have with God. I encourage you to rejoice in this love and accept this precious love. As you walk through life, just let the joy of the Lord be your strength (Nehemiah 8:10). Walk joyfully and happily knowing who you are in Christ, no matter what the circumstance around you may be.

The days of God's princess walking around with her head down are over. You are to let the world see the change in you and give God the glory. The days of feeling less than, discouraged and defeated, and second-rate are gone. You are a child of the Most High. You are His princess. Allow Him to place a new glow and joy around you that will be evident to all.

Read and write Psalms 143:8.

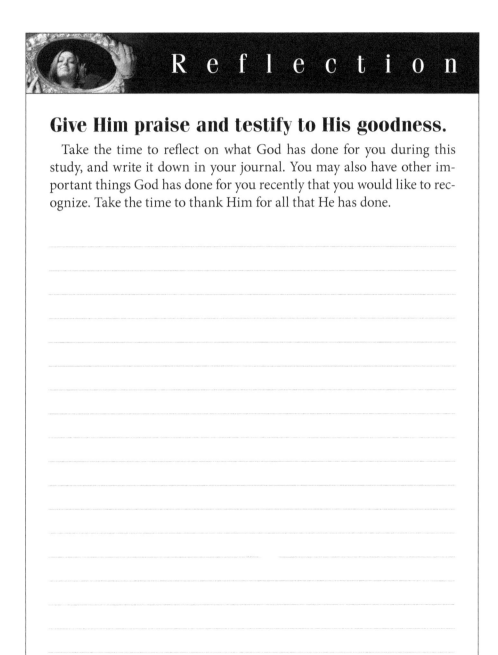

Reflection

Give Him praise and testify to His goodness.

Take the time to reflect on what God has done for you during this study, and write it down in your journal. You may also have other important things God has done for you recently that you would like to recognize. Take the time to thank Him for all that He has done.

Prayer Time

Dear Heavenly Father,

Thank you Jesus for my new clothes! Thank you for my royal wardrobe that you have adorned me with. Help me to wear it with strength, honor, and dignity. Help me to represent you well. Show me areas that do not. Help me to be dressed as the princess of God you have created me to be, in Jesus name. – Amen

Day 4

Beauty Is In You!

In this step, you have focused on being a beautiful princess of God. You are beautiful, and you need to know that in your heart. The beauty that God sees is not what the world sees as beauty. He looks at the heart not at the outward appearance. The world has put so much pressure on women to be "beautiful" on the outside. Women struggle with diets and surgeries trying to make themselves something by the world's standards. You can tell by looking at any magazine at the checkout stand. When the inner beauty is discovered and there is peace and happiness inside, the outside appearance is taken care.

First of all, as a woman who is healed of self-esteem issues (you notice my wording here, you are healed in Jesus name), you must recognize that you are beautiful on the inside. Jesus Christ is resident in you, and you share in His glory and beauty. Recognize yourself as beautiful because you were created by God to be a masterpiece. He created you "good", and you are beautiful to Him. You will need to align both the inside beauty and outward beauty with God's word.

⠿ Read and write 1 Peter 3:3-4.

_____

_____

_____

_____

There is nothing you can do to make yourself more beautiful to God if you have accepted Jesus Christ, and are dedicating your life to following His word. God is not concerned with all the "extras" women do to themselves. He looks directly at your heart to see your character, your Christ-like attitude, and the fruit of your life. Does all this mean that you can not dress up with nice clothes, jewelry, and do your hair nice? Certainly not! You should always be the best that you can with what you have. Take care of what God has given you. Remember that your heart is where your real beauty is found, and that is of great worth to God.

:: Read and write Romans 12:1.

_____

_____

_____

_____

_____

You may base a lot of the way that you feel about yourself on your body and what you see. I think it is important to realize that we need to take care of our bodies. Your body is the only one that you will have, and there will not be a second chance to take better care of it. Your body is God's temple. You are a living sacrifice for Him. Everything you do, what you eat, how you exercise, rest, work, wear your makeup, and even how you dress is a spiritual act of worship to God. Your smile, countenance, disposition, temperament, manners, attitude, and talk are all spiritual acts of worship to Him.

It is up to you to take the body that God has given you and do your very best with it. You need to be careful of what you do with your body. Your body is a reflection of Christ because He lives within you. This is a much deeper topic than this study can cover, but I do want to encourage you to take good care of what God has given you. Everything you do to your body, you do to Him because He lives in you. If you walk around mad and with a bad attitude, you are representing Him. How are your true spiritual acts of worship today?

As a princess of God, He that lives in you is greater than He that is in the world. You do not need to seek the things of this world, but to be _transformed allowing your mind to be renewed_ (Romans 12:2 paraphrased). You are beautiful, and all the beauty you need is within you. Be the best that you can possibly be for the glory of God. You are His glory!

Time to Journal

What can you do to better represent Christ in your appearance? You can do things as simple as these listed here: smiling more to reflect His joy, dressing neater and showing that you do care about yourself, getting proper exercise and eating right. What is it for you?

Prayer Time

Dear Heavenly Father,

Thank you for my body. Thank you that you live in me! Lead me in the way that I need to go to be a pleasing sacrifice for you. Help all of my actions, thoughts, words, appearance, and management of my body be a good spiritual act of worship. I pray that the Holy Spirit would strengthen me in this area and teach me, correct me, and lead me in the right way. I need your grace and love to be the temple you desire. Forgive me for falling short in this area. Help me to be beautiful within and reflect your beauty on the outside, in Jesus name. – Amen

Day 5

Love And Accept Yourself

> *But who are you, O man, to talk back to God? Shall what is formed say to him who formed it, "Why did you make me like this?"*
>
> – Romans 9:20

I know you are probably thinking how can I love myself? I do not mean to love yourself in a prideful way, but I do believe that you are to love yourself. The Bible tells us that we are to love everybody, and I believe that includes you. You can never get away from you. Loving yourself is hard to do, but possible. Some of you are probably thinking "I don't even like myself." Well, you are now "new"! You have been changed. Beware of the thoughts that try to tell you differently. That is the old you, and you have been made new. Why not love you? You were created by God! Read His word and I think that you will get my point.

This scripture speaks so boldly for itself. As a woman, you must accept what God created you to be. He is pleased. Who are you to question the Potter? He created the earth in its fullness, and He created you too. You are a miracle creation of God. When God created you, He knew the color of your eyes, hair, skin tone, and even how tall you would be. You were like clay in the Potter's hand. He shaped, molded, and fashioned you to be what He desired. When you look in the mirror and say "I don't like what I see." You are talking about God's creation, and you are talking about the One who lives within you. Accept how God created you and who He created you to be today.

He is faithful!

I praise God for His wonderful work that I know He has accomplished in you during this study. God is an awesome God, and *He* is a faithful God. I hope that you are praising Him along with me for the healing process He has brought you through. I am rejoicing for you! Ladies, you are free in Christ to *be* whoever God has purposed you to be. It is time for you to take your place in Christ. Rejoice in His faithfulness, as *He will never leave you nor forsake you* (Hebrews13:5).

:: Read and write Psalms 145:13.

_____

_____

_____

He is faithful to all generations, and He is the same yesterday, and today, and forever (Hebrews 13:8). He is faithful to restore and to heal you. If you will surrender and walk victoriously, your self-esteem will never be the same. The Lord will keep His promise to you. I know in my heart that God is rejoicing with us this day over the restoration in His precious daughter, _____, and the and the princess that she is going to rise up to be! Worship with your Joy. *For the joy of the Lord is your strength.* Nehemiah 8:10b

As a woman of God, you are special to your heavenly Father, and you must receive that. You must also come to know you are special in your heart. You will never find another love and relationship like the one you can have with God. I encourage you to rejoice in this love and accept this precious love. As you walk through life, let the joy of the Lord be your strength (Neh. 8:10). Walk joyfully and happily knowing who you are in Christ no matter what the circumstances around you.

:: Read and write Psalms 126:3.

_____

_____

_____

_____

_____

Prayer Time

Dear Heavenly Father,

Forgive me when I have complained or questioned your creation. I know that you are faithful and everything that you have created is good. You will lead me in the way to trust you and grow in my walk with you. Thank you for showing me who I am in you. Help me to remember your word as truth and to reflect on it daily. Help me to love and accept myself as you have accepted me. Lead me to another level in my self-esteem healing. Help me, O Lord, to apply your word for my life and for my self-esteem. I pray that I may bring you glory and others can witness your great works in me. I pray that others may see my new joy that only comes from you. I pray that my new self-esteem will be contagious to other women! Open my eyes and my heart to grow in you. I desire to never go back to the old way I used to be. Help me to think differently about myself. Help me to see more of you when I look in the mirror and to be pleased with what I see. I need you Lord. I want you in my life, in my self-esteem. Thank you for healing me. I realize that you are not finished with me yet. Help me, Lord, to always be in touch with the Holy Spirit. Help me to listen to who you say I am and not the lies. Help me in the days to come to be armed for the battle when tough times come. You are my strength and my Rock. You are my peace, and I trust you. Help me to keep my mind on you and pursue peace all the days of my life. I believe that I am free to be all that you created me to be. I am special, and I am a princess of God. I love you, and I thank you, in Jesus name! – Amen

Prayer Time

Step Seven
The Beauty of It All!

You are healed in Jesus name!

I believe that this is your defining moment to receive from Jesus. Trust in Him because He has led you to where you are right now. He paid the price for you with such a deep love that you will never understand it all until you meet Him. It is time that you realize the great price He paid for you to be healed. When He came, Jesus came for a purpose to be fulfilled. As you read the last few passages, I encourage you to open you heart and receive everything He came for. He went to the cross for your healing, and it is your defining moment to receive.

Read and write Isaiah 53:4-5.

_____

_____

_____

_____

_____

Read and write Psalms 107:20.

_____

_____

_____

_____

He sent *His word* to heal you! The *word* became flesh, and His name is Jesus. He went to the cross so that you could be healed and made whole. He took the stripes for the healing of your body, mind, and soul. You are made whole and healed in Jesus name. When Jesus was on the cross, He thought of you, and gave His life for you. The punishment and suffering that was upon Him was needed for your peace and well-being. He sent His word for you to have perfect constant peace in *Him.*

I truly believe that God sent this study your way to open your eyes to see what He has done for you. Jesus paid a great price for you. You are co-heirs with Jesus, and you are a child of God. God is calling you to a higher level. Jesus did not go to the cross for you to live a defeated life. He went to the cross so that you could be victorious!

God is calling His daughters to seek Him, and let Him accomplish all that He has for you. No longer are you to hang your head in shame and defeat, but you are to rise up from the grave! Psalms 107:20, NIV says, *He sent forth His word and healed them; he rescued them from the grave.* Hallelujah! My dear sister in the Lord, He has sent His word to rescue you from the grave. He is standing before you, calling you to come forth and be healed in Jesus name. Rise up! Come forth in Jesus name! Princess _____ , you are healed from a low self-esteem in Jesus name! In faith, receive your healing and give God all the glory for He is a faithful!

Encouragement for you

As this study comes to an end, I pray that you would remember God's word. Let the peace of Christ rule in you. This study has taken you to a lot of scripture that tells you who you are in Christ. You have faced a lot of bondages, mind battles, struggles, strongholds, unforgiveness, and weaknesses. You have been through such a healing process. I want to encourage you to never go back to where you were. Look to Jesus and keep your eyes set on what is in front of you. Hebrews 12:2 says, *Fix your eyes on Jesus.*

> *Forgetting what is behind and straining toward what is ahead.*
>
> – (Philippians 3:13, paraphrased).

Stand firm on His word and meditate on it daily. He sent His word to heal you, and I encourage you to grow in the word. It is time for you to walk forward with Christ and rise up to be the woman of God he intended you to be. This is your defining moment in your life with the Lord. You go from this moment forward to all that God has for you. You are His princess! Give Him praise and honor for the healing within you. He deserves your highest praise!

My Prayer For You

I pray in Jesus name that out of his glorious riches he may strengthen you with power through his spirit in your inner being, so that Christ may dwell in your hearts through faith. I pray that you being rooted and established in love, may have power, together with all the saints, to grasp how wide and how long and high and deep is the love of Christ, and to know this love that surpasses knowledge, that you may be filled to the measure of all the fullness of God. Now to Him who is able to do immeasurably more than all we ask or imagine, according to his power that is at work within us, to Him be the glory, in Jesus name, Amen

– (Ephesians 3:16-21a).

Now if we are children, then we are heirs-heirs of God and co-heirs with Christ.

– Romans 8:17

So if the Son sets you free, you will be free indeed.

– John 8:36

So, _____, if the Son has set you free, then Princess _____, you are indeed free. Princess _____, you have a healthy self-esteem in Jesus name. You are co-heirs with Christ. You are free to be whatever God has purposed you to be.

Rejoice in the Lord!

Step Eight
The Reward

You have just completed an awesome healing journey. Praise God! I want to encourage you to reward yourself. Treat yourself as the princess of God that you are. Take time alone with God to thank him for all that He has done in you. Take time to pamper yourself and take care of your body. I have some suggestions that I like below. This is your reward, but don't let it stop here, it must continue daily!

1. Treat yourself to a Day Spa or do a home spa for yourself.

2. Take yourself to dinner or invite your husband out to celebrate.

3. Throw a self-esteem party. Maybe invite some other women with healthy esteem to celebrate with you.

4. Get yourself a crown! Wear it on days that you are struggling. You are a princess so wear the crown.

5. Buy yourself a beautiful rose or your favorite flower. Remind yourself each time you look at it that you are as beautiful as that rose God created.

Write Jesus a love letter expressing your new found freedom in your self-esteem.

Dear Jesus,

Love,
Your Princess

You are free!

You too are *fearfully and wonderfully made,* and you too are a princess of the King. It is time for you to live free and walk into your rightful place in the King's Court. Jesus Christ is the King, and you are the princess. I encourage you to become deep rooted in the love that He has for you and to seek Him daily as you grow to be the free princess that He created you to be. *Be Free in Jesus name!*

Living free as a Princess of the King!

With Love,
Lesia

Step Nine
Free To Be A Princess!

Testimony of Princess Cindy Whitlock

"Free to Be a Princess".....This Bible study has ministered to me in so many ways. I had the privilege of reading the study while it was a work in progress. Even then, I began the self-esteem healing process. As I helped Lesia with editing and proofreading, like comas or misspelled words, what I read was helping me all the more! As I read and took every word to heart, some-thing started to change in me. I found that I wasn't just looking for errors I was being changed! I started to realize who I was in Christ. Very important! I am a child of God! That makes me His princess! That just makes me excited with a joy that I would love to share with you!

It would take a lot of pages for me to go into detail about my self-esteem, but I will give you the highlights. I have hated my body because of being overweight. I hated the miserable person I was inside because of it. And there are many issues with my past that I won't go into since that would be a whole other book itself. I had to make the decision to take some action and follow this Bible study and change a lot of my mindsets and realize who I am in Christ. In Christ, I am an heir of God and co-heirs with Christ, I have had to completely change the way I see myself and began looking at myself through the eyes of God. It was then that everything began to change and I started to look and feel precious to my heavenly Father.

Ladies, I must tell you that it was not easy to go through this process, but you have to go "through" in order to make progress. I discovered that I am Princess Cindy. I am His princess! Everything that is God's is mine and all of His promises are "yes' and "amen". I am a beautiful child of God. I do not have to live in bondage anymore; the past is the past. I have power over Satan in the name of Jesus, and I intend to use it in the name of Jesus! I intend to walk in that power and live victoriously. Ladies, I encourage you not to allow Satan to control your thoughts. You can learn ways through this study to recognize the tricks of the enemy and live in victory.

I encourage you to allow God to have freedom to work in your life through this study. I want for you to know who you are in Christ. You too are a princess and you are a beautiful child of God. I thank God for this study and the healing that I received. Thank you, Lesia, for allowing God to work through you in writing "Free to Be a Princess". My self-esteem is higher because of it, and I am *Free To Be A Princess!*

With Love,

Cindy Whitlock
Princess of the King

Testimony of Princess Melanie McConnell

What God has done in my life is absolutely amazing! The words can only portray a picture in your mind, but could never show the depth of how much God (through this Bible study) has truly "marked" my life forever!

I was raised in a good Christian home and was made to go to church. I heard the story of baby Jesus, Noah's Ark, Crucifixion, and Resurrection of Jesus Christ. I heard it all! I memorized so many Bible verses that I probably knew the Bible from front to back.

I am 31 years old and have spent the last 12 years of my life with depression, condemnation, low self-esteem, past guilt, hurts, and feelings of worthlessness and the list goes on and on! I just thought as a Christian I would just have to deal with these things as best I could.

When I started this study there was such an anointing over it that right from the beginning it overflowed into my life. I had to make up my own mind that no matter what I had to dig up, lay down, or give up, I would do it and I could be an over comer! Once I got started into the study, I found that I had a lot of issues with myself. Some I knew about and was ready to deal with, but others I had buried a long time ago and I was not ready to deal with. At first, I was coming into this study just thinking that I was going to get some self-esteem. I did get that, but I also had past sins to deal with and past hurts to deal with. I had to deal with people that I thought that I had forgiven, but had not and there were other specifics that are too personal to go into.

For the first time, Bible verses that I had heard over and over again became real to my life. I learned how to apply them to my life and myself. I always thought that things like joy, peace, patience, self-worth, and confidence belonged to others. I felt as if there were only a chosen few who had joy and all the others were supposed to be miserable. The change came in my mind when I started believing and repeatedly telling myself throughout everyday that I was going to have all that God had promised me. It was then that I began to see myself change. For the first time in my life I can say that I love myself! I am still very hard on myself, but I have come so far and overcome a lot of junk! When I look in the mirror I don't see someone I hate because there is so much more of "Him" in me that it is getting harder to see myself! It's all for His glory, not mine! I have to continually pray and offer up praises to Him because the more I try the harder the enemy tries to change my mind. As long as I keep my thoughts continuously set on Him, my enemies are being cast down!

One of the biggest revelations I had was in Psalms 139:13-14. *For you have created my inmost being; you knit me together in my mother's womb. I praise you because "I am fearfully and wonderfully made, your works are wonderful I know that full well* (paraphrased). Through this verse I realized that in my mother's womb, He made me exactly the way He wanted me to be. He loves me just the way I am- faults included! He doesn't expect me to be perfect; He just wants me to strive to BE! I enjoy life now because I know that it is what God wants for me. I still struggle with things, but thank God I don't live in my struggles anymore. True faith in God is believing and speaking into existence what hasn't happened yet!! I am on my way!

Living Free,

Melanie McConnell
Princess of the King

Scripture Cards

*On the next page, cut out the cards so that you can meditate on key scriptures from this study. It's important to keep the word of God before you as you begin to heal.

Cut along the dotted lines.

...to bestow on them a crown of beauty instead of ashes, the oil of gladness instead of mourning, and a garment of praise instead of a spirit of despair. They will be called oaks of righteousness, a planting of the Lord for the display of his splendor.

– Isaiah 61:3

Yet, O Lord, You are our Father, We are the clay, You are the potter; we are all the work of your hand.

– Isaiah 64:8

For you created my inmost being; you knit me together in my mother's womb. I praise you because I am fearfully and wonderfully made; your works are wonderful, I know that full well.

– Psalms 139:13-14

So if the Son sets you free, you will be free indeed.

– John 8:36

Now if we are children, then we are heirs-heirs of God and co-heirs with Christ, if indeed we share in his sufferings in order that we may also share in his glory.

– Romans 8:17

How great is the love the Father has lavished on us, that we should be called children of God. And that is what we are!...

– 1 John 3:1a

Your kingdom is an everlasting kingdom, and your dominion endures through all generations. The Lord is faithful to all his promises and loving toward all he has made.

– Psalms 145:13

And we know that in all things God works for the good of those who love him, who have been called according to his purpose.

– Romans 8:28

For we are God's workmanship, created in Christ to do good works, which God prepared in advance for us to do.

– Ephesians 2:10

The Lord your God is with you, he is mighty to save. He will take great delight in you, he will quiet you with his love, he will rejoice over you with singing.

– Zephaniah 3:17

Contact Us

I pray that this study has been a blessing to you. If you would like to contact Lesia Glick for more information, a speaking engagement, or to receive additional copies of this study, please write or e-mail us at:

Lesia Glick
www.lesiaglick.com
email: freetobe@lesiaglick.com

Be Free!

CPSIA information can be obtained
at www.ICGtesting.com
Printed in the USA
LVHW061339160519
618096LV00015B/350/P